COMMON SENSE OF CONTEMPORARY AMERICAN ECONOMICS AND POLITICS

HOW AMERICA COULD BECOME A TRUE DEMOCRACY

KURT LEWIS ALLEN

authorHOUSE®

AuthorHouse™ LLC
1663 Liberty Drive
Bloomington, IN 47403
www.authorhouse.com
Phone: 1-800-839-8640

Published by AuthorHouse 07/07/2014

ISBN: 978-1-4969-2459-9 (sc)
ISBN: 978-1-4969-2458-2 (e)

Library of Congress Control Number: 2014912085

To my loving wife, Debbie, your faith and continuing encouragement have helped me put into words the ideas and concepts I have spent most of my life developing. Without your support, this project may never have been completed.

An Economy is nothing more than an accumulation of Goods and Services. The labor expended to provide the Goods and Services entitles the laborer to extract a like amount of Goods and Services from the Economy. Money is nothing more than a marker of expended labor.

CONTENTS

INTRODUCTION

Economic theories presuppose that the consumer has money to spend on goods and services. However, business owners, who supply the goods and services of the economy, notoriously underpay their employees, who are also the consumer, in an effort to maximize profits. Consumer credit is required to temporarily provide a path to keep the economy afloat. Unfortunately, consumer credit results in a downward spiral of the economy, and the economy eventually crashes. The crashes have been observed throughout history and generally result in a correction to the theories of economic systems. Heretofore, the underlying problem, insufficient funds in the hands of the consumer, seems to have escaped the notice of those manipulating the complex calculations.

In order to have an economic system that works, it is necessary to assure that every adult who wants a job can have a job that pays a living wage.

Minimum wage laws have so far proved to be more problematic than successful. First of all, no minimum wage has ever equated to a living wage. Secondly, employers routinely find ways to circumvent the minimum wage laws.

Action rather than force of law is the answer to this age-old problem. The government needs to provide a job that pays, at a minimum, a living wage to every adult who wants a job. By doing this, every business owner who needs employees to acquire profit from his or her business will be forced to pay no less than a living wage to his or her employees.

Throughout history, governments have taxed their citizens to pay the wages of their employees. This practice would lead one to believe that government employee labor has no value of its own and can only receive value from the labor or business of private citizens. Nothing can be further from the truth. In fact, a country's value is derived in part from the results of the labor of the citizens who work for their government. This value can be calculated and quantified and then used to fund an account from which government labor can be paid. *To preclude devastating effects to a nation's economy, the labor-supported money that funds the account can only be used to pay government labor.*

The value added to the country by each government employee's labor is rarely if ever equal to the wages paid to the employee. In some cases the value is higher than the wages paid and in some cases lower or quite possibly nonexistent. The quantifying and calculating of the value of each government job is done and termed as a coefficient to the wage earned by each laborer performing that job. And then the earned wage is multiplied by the coefficient and deposited to an account within the government from which only the wages earned by government employees is taken. At any time the account reaches a zero balance, then it will be necessary to pay government employee wages with collected taxes until the funds in the account again rise. *The collected tax dollars used to pay government labor can never be paid back to the general fund because this very action will open the door to abuse.*

Excess funds in the account can grow to infinity with no damage to the economy or burden on the account. After all, it is only numbers, and if the country's value is increased far above the cost of the labor expended to increase its value, all is well. Take money from this account for other purposes or for the inflated salaries of elected officials and the premise on which this innovation is built will be destroyed. In all likelihood the balance in this account, once well established, will hover well into the positive but nowhere near infinity.

This addition to economic principles will pay for the manpower to provide needed government services without a corresponding tax drain on the economy, but more importantly it will create a situation where business owners will need to pay their employees, at a minimum, a living wage or suffer the consequences of having no employees.

Initially businesses with employees may need to increase the price of their product in order to meet payroll and still maintain a profit, but the payment of no less than a living wage to every adult who wants a job will assure that there are customers who can afford the product at its increased price. Granted the concept in theory could create an ever-escalating spiral of wages and prices in order to maintain a living wage, but in all likelihood it will not take long for business owners to realize it is in their best interest to seek a balance and stay there.

The idea that every adult that wants a job needs to have a job that pays a living wage may be a new concept to those that form and analyze the theories of economics, but it is a well-known fact to every working-class person the world over. It is also a fact that for every action there is a reaction.

This book was conceived to present and defend the premise that government labor has value that can be used to justify the printing of money with which the wages of government labor can be paid. Applying this concept can pave the way to assuring that every adult that wants a job can have a job that pays, at a minimum, a living wage—an action and a reaction both positive.

In researching the facts and theories of economics, I have become aware of many not-so-positive actions of big business and government (which at this point in time seem to be one and the same) that have decidedly negative reactions. After sharing the detriments of our present economic and political situation, I will suggest many positive actions that are meant to create equally positive reactions for big business, small business, government, and, most importantly, the people.

CHAPTER 1

BANKS

A large portion of every working person's paycheck, with few exceptions, is needed to pay for living expenses. The remainder of each paycheck is generally not enough to pay for large ticket items such as automobiles. Unexpected expenses, such as car repairs, can easily exceed the remains of one paycheck. In order to make large purchases or pay for unexpected expenses, people need to have money set aside. Businesses, like the individuals they employ, also need to set money aside for unexpected expenses and large purchases.

Burying coffee cans filled with money in the back yard is probably not the best solution. Banks are a much better option. First of all, banks are more secure and easier to find. Secondly, a portion of the money deposited by individuals and businesses is available for the bank to loan.

There are times when a business is confronted with an unexpected expense that exceeds the money the business has available in savings. The business manager must decide whether the business can put off the expense until the business has saved enough cash to pay the expense or if the business should borrow the money needed from the bank. To make this decision, the business owner must consider certain facts: Will the unpaid expense put them out of business? Can the business afford the additional monthly bill that will be generated to repay the loan with interest?

A business owner may be confronted with an opportunity to expand the business and thereby increase the business's income. The expansion may take more money than the business owner has available in savings. The business manager must decide whether to wait until money is available in cash to expand the business or whether the business should borrow the money from the bank and expand the business now. To make the decision the business manager must consider: Will the increased income be more than enough to make the monthly payments on the loan, which will include interest? Will the opportunity for expansion and thereby increased income wait until the money can be saved? What is the break-even point between the sum total of the added monthly income minus the debt payment starting now and the sum total of the added income starting when the money for expansion is saved?

In both examples above, the smart business manager only takes out a loan when he or she knows the loan payment is going to be paid in full with profits that would not be available without the loan.

An individual can also borrow money from a bank, but in no case can those payments in effect pay for themselves, so the smart individual never borrows money. It is far better for an individual's long-term financial benefit to wait until he or she can save enough money to make the purchase in cash, because credit creates a monthly payment with interest, which takes up a portion of future paychecks.

At this point, many people will want to argue that it is not possible to buy a house without a loan. My answer to that argument is, "It used to be and still would be possible for the average person to buy a house with cash if the first individuals to buy a house with credit had made the decision to wait until they saved the cash needed to buy a house." In our present economic condition, you can add automobiles and, it seems, everything else to our list of things that are not possible to buy without credit.

Banks are places where the working person and business can deposit money in savings so the accumulated money will be available for special or emergency purchases. Banks use a portion of the money on deposit to make loans to businesses that need extra funds to pay for unexpected expenses or expansion of the business. Banks may also finance the start up of a new business.

The business owners return the money in small increments with interest until their loan is paid in full. The interest paid covers the bank's operating expenses, plus some profit.

As a service to their customers banks offer checking accounts, where workers and businessmen alike can temporarily place their income and then authorize the bank to distribute funds by use of a check, debit card, or electronic request.

CHAPTER 2

INVESTMENT BANKS

Investment banks raise money for governments by buying and selling issues of their bonds and raise money for corporations by buying and selling issues of their stock or bonds.

Governments incur an almost immediate drain from their treasury in the form of interest from the issuance of bonds and a future debt that must be paid from their treasury for the repayment of the principle of the bonds. The nation's treasury obviously wasn't big enough to support the government to begin with, so where are the extra funds for, interest on, and repayment of, the bonds going to come from?

Debt is never a good option for a government. It has been used throughout the centuries because the nation's rich, who seem to always gain control over their government, can loan money to their government by buying government bonds and then collecting interest on the investment of their money rather than paying taxes to finance their government. The payment of taxes equates to transferring of money out of the control of the individual and into the control of the government. The rich individuals place themselves in a position to prevent that transference of money from their pocket, which increases the amount of money each working class person has removed from his or her pocket.

The incurrence of debt by a nation's government to a nation's rich citizens is a travesty against that nation's working class citizens because the working class ends up paying for the entire cost of the country's operating expenses plus the cost of paying profits in the form of interest to the rich. The expense cannot be indefinitely borne by the working class and eventually results in a downward spiral of the nation's economy through a lack of consumer spending.

The lack of consumer spending eventually leads to a shortage of money available to the nation's rich citizens and opens the door for sale of a nation's government bonds outside the country. This has become such a common occurrence in our global economy that it is taken for granted.

The real danger, however, is when a nation's government becomes indebted to the government of another nation. Bonds are only issued by countries that practice capitalism. Communist governments own everything within their country so the profits of industry automatically flow into the government treasury. A country with adequate financial resources to buy up a substantial portion of another country's debt, both private, in the form of individual and business loans, and public, in the form of government bonds, and in addition buys up a mass quantity of a country's currency, gains title to the other country. At the point where the indebted nation's government and its people find it impossible to make payments on the loans, the door is opened to foreclosure, but, of course, the loaning nation's government would need a police force the size of an army to actually foreclose on the borrowing nation.

Investment banks increase their riches by enlarging the national debt of governments controlled by the rich, but their real niche is funding the creation and growth of corporations. A person or persons with an idea for a business can go to an investment bank with the idea. If the bank thinks there is enough merit in the idea for investors to buy stock, then it will put together a package for the sale of stock, sell the stock, and take its fee from the sale. The bankers may even buy some of the stock themselves.

Once a corporation is established and sees an opportunity for increasing sales through expansion by building a larger business establishment or more business establishments or maybe by buying out a competitor, the corporation can get the funds needed by going back to the investment bank. The bank will sit down with the corporate leaders and decide whether it is best to sell more stock, which increases the number of owners of the corporation, or sell bonds, which creates debt for the corporation.

If the corporation increases the number of owners through the sale of new stock, then the expansion needs to produce enough added income to pay all the owners (old stockholders and new) more dividends than the original stockholders were receiving prior to the sale of new stock. In addition, the value of each share of stock must, in a reasonable amount of time, increase above the price it was at prior to the sale of the new stock.

If both of these conditions are not assured, then the bank and corporate leaders may decide on the issuance of bonds. It would be better for the corporate entity to save the money for expansion rather than borrow it through the sale of bonds, but in order to save the money, the corporation would have to deny the stockholders dividends while it saved enough money from its profits. The stockholders (owners of the corporation) don't care about what is best for the corporate entity; they invested in the corporation to make money, so they want their dividends.

The investment bankers don't care about the corporate entity either; they are in business to make money, and it doesn't matter whether they sell stock or bonds. The sale of either makes them money. Investment banks thrive on the creation and expansion of corporations. In truth, neither the owners nor the financiers of a corporation care about the corporation; they just want it to grow so they can make more money.

The quality of the goods or service provided by the corporation to make its profits likewise has no importance to the owners and financiers as long as the customer buys the corporation's product. If there is a problem with getting the customer to buy the product of the corporation, then the decision may be made by the corporate leaders to improve the quality of the product. The corporate leaders may instead decide to lower the price of the product. In some cases the corporate leadership may solve the problem by buying out the competition, which has a better product and is making sales. After the sale, the corporate leaders may substitute the superior product in the marketplace for their inferior product or use the design of the superior product to increase the quality of their existing product. The corporate leaders will take the cheapest course of action to maintain or increase profits. The corporate owners will support the corporate leaders' decision, and the investment bank will be happy to finance the decision as long as they all make more money.

The owners of the corporation, who care nothing for the company they own and who simply want their dividends and the ability to sell their stock for more than they bought it for, care even less for the customer than they do for their company. The employees of the corporation, of course, are cared about the least. If they are thought of at all by the owners, it is as a drain on corporate profits.

Because of the economy of scale afforded large companies, such as corporations, it is hard for small companies to compete with them. The small company usually cannot afford the machinery a large company may use in place of manpower. The small company also pays more for its raw materials because it buys its materials in smaller quantities. In order to compete in the marketplace the small company must make a better product because with its increased manpower costs and raw material cost it usually has no choice but to charge a higher price for its product, and the customer will only pay the higher price if he or she can justify the higher price by acquiring a better product.

Competition between small companies results in even higher quality products because the company with the higher-quality product is going to enjoy a larger share of the market. Small manufacturing companies open the door to small raw material companies. Small retail companies open the door to small manufacturing companies. Small companies are of no use to corporations because they cannot supply the needs of the corporation.

Small companies tend to treat their employees better than do large companies because with fewer employees it is easier for top management, which usually includes the company's owner, to know all of the employees personally.

Traditional local banks can serve small companies. Investment banks have no interest in small businesses, unless they are trying to turn themselves into a large corporation.

Elected officials regularly spout their reason for giving tax breaks to large businesses as being the fact that big businesses provide needed jobs. The truth is big businesses pay for campaigns and lobbying. Large business uses machinery to replace workers much more often than do small businesses. It takes many small businesses to manufacture an equal quantity of goods as one large business. One corporate store takes the place of many small stores. Many corporate stores limit the hours of their employees to eliminate the need of paying for benefits and in addition rarely pay their workers a living wage. Most small stores are owner-operated. Family members regularly participate in the business. Many small stores are large enough to have a few employees. These employees are treated much better than they would be if they were employed at a corporate store.

Small businesses collectively used to employ far more workers than large businesses. However, because of the economy of scale it is difficult for small companies to compete with large incorporated companies, and when you take into account the tax breaks afforded to large business, it is impossible for small businesses to compete with them.

The investment bank is a tool of corporations. Corporations are the bread and butter of investment banks. It is a symbiotic relationship made in stockholder heaven. To help themselves grow, investment banks seek out opportunities to create new corporations and help existing corporations to grow. Corporations are growing bigger and bigger. In the process, they are swallowing each other through acquisitions and mergers financed by the investment banks.

The consumers and employees alike are suffering in the process. The goods and services provided to the customers by these conglomerates are of poor quality at best. Many of the cheaper products are designed to break. The more expensive products, which are also designed to break, can only be repaired by workers of the conglomerate who have the needed specialized tools at their disposal and have been trained to do the work, which by design has been made complicated and requires specialized tools.

Airline passengers pay top dollar for a seat they can barely fit into and, after being stuffed into airplanes like sardines, are charged extra for every possible service.

Many of the more subtle ways in which we are all negatively affected by corporations with their easy access to money are shown and discussed in subsequent chapters.

Without investment banks, a business could only grow through customer support, and it would only get that support through customer satisfaction. Corporations would need to stay in business long enough to save the money required for expansion, and to do that they would need to maintain satisfied customers.

Investment banks eliminate customer votes
and place nations in grave danger.

CHAPTER 3

BREEDING MONEY

The accumulated interest paid to creditors in most cases exceeds the original principle loaned before a debt is ever paid in full. As the interest rolls in, it is sent back out as principle on a new loan so that the collected interest can produce interest.

Loaning money has become big business. It requires no machinery, raw materials, or warehouse space. The overhead is low, and the profits are massive. To avoid high taxes, the overhead is boosted by paying enormous salaries to the top echelons, furnishing offices with immaculate décor, providing private jets for executive travel, and many other unnecessary "business expenses."

Charging interest on a loan, is it legal theft or just good business? The Bible says, "If you lend money to one of my people among you who is needy, do not treat it like a business deal; charge no interest" (Exodus 22:25).

Creditors could argue that by demanding proof of the ability to repay a loan before loaning money, they are assured of never loaning money to the needy. Simply by observing what has transpired over the past forty years, I would have to differ with them. Granted most, but not all, people are financially stable before they are issued a credit card, but many of those who start off financially stable soon lose their stability when faced with ever-rising credit card bills.

Credit cards are not the only way in which creditors take advantage of working class citizens. House loans, although very common today, have only been around for slightly longer than credit cards. In fact, it has become a requirement to have well-established credit through the use of credit cards before a loan for a house will be granted.

My grandfather, a factory worker at the C&H sugar refinery, saved until he had enough money to purchase a house. My mother, her sister, and two brothers were born and grew up in the house my grandfather paid for with cash. Today a worker with a similar job could start saving when he was single and save until his children had grown children of their own and still not be able to purchase a house in cash.

Granted inflation has increased the price of everything, but it has also increased the wages of workers. So it stands to reason that it should still be possible for a worker to save enough money to buy a house in cash. Why isn't it? The answer is that house prices have increased far more than the rate of inflation. The accelerated increase in the price of houses is not an accident. It is a planned event, and the availability of credit for the purpose of buying a house is the tool used to bring about this phenomenon.

Some very greedy bankers, using their political influence gained through campaign contributions, got legislation passed that allowed them to increase the percentage of customer deposits they could loan. The loan of excess money allowed the bank to make more profit. Before the increase, the funds that could be loaned were a smaller percentage of the cash on deposit, and this allowed loans for business only. Increased availability of money to loan created the availability to loan money for nonbusiness purposes, such as home loans.

Offering to loan money to a borrower who was saving for a home made sense for the borrower as well as for the bank. The borrower could have his home immediately, and the bank could profit from the interest income. The banks, as well as the depositors, were protected by the fact that real estate was easily resold if the borrower could not make his payments.

Housing loans proved to be a safe, lucrative way to loan money. The banks, again using their political influence, pushed the idea that it was the right of every American to purchase their own home. Some deregulation of the banking laws freed up funds and allowed more people to acquire loans than ever before. The cost of houses increased with the increase in demand.

It didn't take long before the down payment needed to purchase a home was equal to the prior total cost of the same home. This made it difficult for many new buyers, but with more deregulation of the banking laws, more funds became available for the banks to use, and the banks created loans with a zero down payment.

As bank profits increased, the banks were able to augment the share of funds on deposit that could be loaned with their own money, gained through interest. This allowed banks to loan even more money and thus collect more interest, which further increased the money they had available to loan. The spiral continued until the banks no longer needed depositors' savings to stay in business, at which time savings accounts no longer had importance to the banks. The banks reduced the percent of interest they paid on savings well below the rate of inflation, and Americans, in general, ceased to save.

The lack of savings created a problem for consumers because purchases requiring funds in excess of the remains of one paycheck were no longer possible. The void was filled by the creation of credit cards. Credit cards made sense for the user as well as the bank. The consumer could again make purchases, which used to be made with savings, and the banks now had another way to loan out money and collect interest on their ever-increasing funds.

The growing funds paid to the bank each month in interest gave the banks sufficient capital to continue giving out loans without needing a significant return from previously loaned principle. The banks in turn decreased the amount of money the borrower was required to pay on the principle each month, which increased the time required for payback and thereby increased the total interest paid. The reduced principle payback required each month reduced monthly payments and allowed users to increase the balance owed on their credit card. The banks happily encouraged this with ever-increasing credit limits. The use of credit cards to pay for purchases has gotten so common that many people have come to think of credit cards as being synonymous with cash money.

Automobile loans are another way banks have of indebting the working class. Automobiles, as with homes, were once purchased with cash. The advent of using credit for their purchase has increased the cost of vehicles far greater than would have been the case based on inflation alone.

The small local banks that make home loans no longer fill the role of mortgage holder. Mortgages are sold to investment banks, sometimes within hours but usually within days of closing. The investment banks that buy the mortgages also buy credit card debt and automobile loans. The sale of these loans frees local banks to extend more credit. The banks sell the loans for more than the face value of the loan because the buyer is entitled to all the interest the loan will generate. The local bank also makes money off the transaction involved with the purchase of the house. The sale of the loan, even before the first mortgage payment is due, means the bank assumes no risk for repayment of the loan. The two profit motives of the local banks together with the elimination of risk make the loan of primary importance and the ability of the borrower to repay the loan of little or no importance.

To fill the high demand for high-interest mortgages, creditors become very creative. They help people into mortgages they can't afford by offering low introductory rates on variable interest loans. Once the debtor has his or her family situated in their new home, the interest rates begin to climb toward the prime interest rate. Once the prime rate is reached, the interest rate continues to grow to make up for the risk involved with loaning money to an individual that for lack of sufficient income or by previous credit history doesn't qualify for a prime interest rate loan.

The duped buyer usually has a variety of options once the house payment reaches its full potential. Their income may have grown to a sufficient level to cover the excessive mortgage payment, in which case they can stay in the house and continue making payments. This is rarely the case. Often the ever-inflating housing market has raised the price of their home to a level that the owner can sell the house and walk away with a profit. The homeowner may also refinance the loan and use the equity to make the house payments. This is the hoped-for outcome because the creditor makes money off the transaction and then gets more money when the new loan is sold. The homeowner may walk away from the home and let the bank repossess it. The homeowner may also stay in the home, stop making payments, and save as much money as possible while the bank goes through foreclosure proceedings. Since the downturn of the housing market starting after 2006, this has been the most common choice.

The Investment banks, after purchasing the loans, bundle them together and sell them for a price higher than the combined principles of all the loans in the bundle. The bundles are carefully put together to assure the average interest rate of the combined loans in the bundle exceeds the average market interest rate. This makes the bundle highly appealing to investors. The investment banker that handles the bundling receives an exorbitant salary plus a massive bonus for making the colossal transaction.

No matter what the choice made by the homeowner, it is of little consequence to the local bank, the investment bank that bought and subsequently sold the mortgage, and, least of all, the banker that placed the loan in a bundle. The owner of the bundle doesn't even feel the pinch if one individual stops making payments on a loan as long as the other debtors in the bundle continue paying the small principle payments on their loan along with the large payments of interest.

Money doesn't just pop into existence. It is supposed to originate with someone making a good or providing a service. The worker providing the good or service wants to plan for the future, so he or she puts a little money away every payday for his or her retirement.

This is where a good portion of the money used to buy these bundled loans comes from.

The managers of the retirement accounts look for investments that pay an interest rate high enough to stay above the inflation rate and return enough income to grow the retirement account to a level that will assure an adequate retirement.

The managers of retirement accounts don't work for free. They regularly take a percentage of each retirement account to cover their fees. A portion of this fee is paid to the trader that manages the account as a salary and a little more is usually paid as a bonus for each transaction that makes a profit. The fees and profits add up to a large sum of money for the management companies. Likewise the salaries and bonuses add up to large sums for the traders.

The traders and management companies alike make investments with their excess income, which is part of their plan for the future. This is where some more of the money comes from for the purchase of the bundled loans. Keep in mind the money these two groups invest originated with the working people who put money away for their retirement.

Another large portion of the money invested in the bundled loans comes from the salaries and bonuses of the employees that put the loan bundles together. Their income is so massive they need to find a place to invest their money or run the risk of losing a portion of the money's value to inflation. They, of course, are also interested in seeing a return, over and above the rate of inflation, on their money.

The rest of the money to purchase the bundled loans comes from rich stockholders and business leaders, all of whom grew their money in various ways, none of which are important at this juncture except to say that their money too originated with the production of a good or provision of a service by many working individuals and not the labor of the investor.

The big bank employees that put the loan bundles together, the traders that manage the retirement accounts, and the rich investors, one and all watch their personal investments very closely, not just looking at them daily but several times daily, and in some cases constantly. They each have the ability to move their money almost instantly through sale of their assets.

Workers with retirement accounts, on the other hand, pay little attention to their accounts. Furthermore, they have little or no immediate control over their assets.

Money doesn't just pop into existence but it sure can pop out of existence or evaporate, as is quite often termed the devaluation of assets.

Subprime is the term used for loans that are given at an interest rate lower than the prime interest rate to individuals who can't afford a loan at the prime rate of interest. These loans are given with an understanding that the rate of interest is variable and will increase. In many cases the understanding is on the part of the bank but not necessarily on the part of the borrower. Let the buyer beware. It really doesn't matter what is said or understood by the bank employee or the borrower. The terms are in writing and fully enforceable. These loans are subject to default at a higher rate than the fixed prime interest rate loans and therefore carry a higher eventual rate of interest.

Credit cards generally carry a rate of interest that equals the prime rate plus a given percentage. The terms are explicitly listed in the provisions of the credit card contract. The more credit-worthy cardholders receive the smaller percentages above prime. The more risky cardholders get higher percentages above prime. The cardholder may be assumed risky by virtue of the fact that they have never before held a credit card. They may also get the higher rate because they have, in the past, been slow to make payment or failed to make payments on previously held credit cards.

New cars are seldom purchased in cash. Car companies often give low interest loans and sometimes zero interest loans to purchasers with good credit ratings. Banks and credit unions also give car loans, usually at a slightly higher rate of interest. Those with poor credit ratings often can only purchase a used car and then usually at an extremely high rate of interest.

Those that issue loans seldom hold them. They sell the loan to large financial institutions and recover the loaned funds with a slight profit. Local banks and credit unions can then make more money issuing new loans. Car dealers need to free up their funds to sell more cars.

The large investment banks bundle subprime home loans, high interest car loans, credit card loans, and other high-interest loans to make a product that will command a high price from an investor. The banks pay high bonuses to the employees that put the bundles together and sell them. The profits made from the sale of the high-interest bundles provide the banks with a massive return on their total investment.

The big banks usually bundle and keep on their books the zero interest car loans, low interest car loans, and prime interest rate home loans because they have a hard time finding a buyer for these bundles that receive a total rate of interest at or below prime. The loans within the bundle are considered safe because they have been given to borrowers that have a high likelihood of repaying the loans. The funds tied up in the loans can be left on the sidelines until the loans are repaid because the bank has increased its operating capital through the profits made on the sale of the high-interest bundles.

The system would seem to be a benefit to all and was indeed highly praised as it evolved. Real estate has always increased in value, and as the system evolved, real estate increased in value faster than any indicators would say it should. Indicators aren't the same as concrete facts and need not be given much heed, especially when massive profits are being made by all.

In 2006, the first sign of a glitch in the system was seen. Real estate prices began to stabilize, and some began to fall. Over time more houses began to lose value. The holders of subprime loans found their sell option and refinance option were no longer available. Instead of one home loan in a bundle ceasing to pay, there were many.

The reduction in house prices reduced the demand for new homes. Craftsmen in the home building industry began being laid off. The reduction of income from paid craftsman to recipient of unemployment insurance eliminated the ability of many credit card holders to make their credit card payment. Used car loans were also in default. Many of the loans that made up the high interest loan bundles began to fail. The rich investors (traders, business leaders, employees of the large bank, retirement account administrators, stockholders), paying close attention to their holdings, sold the high interest loan bundles as fast as they could. The bundles lost value rapidly. Retirement accounts bottomed out, leaving millions of workers without a retirement.

The debtors, paying on the presumed safe loans making up the low interest bearing bundles held by the large investment banks, began defaulting on their loans as their jobs disappeared. The large banks found themselves in severe financial difficulty. They used their immense political clout, formed by years of campaign contributions, to persuade our country's leaders to loan them the money to regain their solvency. The country, of course, had to borrow money to loan to the banks. So the people of this country who are in debt to the banks for an overpriced house they have in many cases already paid for at least once with money that was credited to interest payments are now further in debt through their future tax liabilities for money that was given to the banks that have enslaved them with financial manipulations.

The bailout has been declared a success, and the large banks are back in business. The financial system has recovered, including, in a big way, the stock market. The developers are getting loans to build houses, homes are being purchased with loans, cars are being financed with loans, and credit cards, which have higher interest rates and new fees, are paying for everything the consumer wants. All the loans, of course, are being bundled for sale to retirement accounts that weren't invested in the bundles on the first go around.

The bailout, however, doesn't seem to be as much of a success for the working class and the still out of work former members of the working class or those that were retired but now because of the loss of their retirement must compete for work. It wouldn't be so bad if the out of work craftsmen that used to build houses could go back to work in the manufacturing jobs from whence they came, but those jobs were shipped overseas at the beginning of the housing boom. Many who didn't lose their homes now owe more on their house than the house is worth. Many house-poor working-class people along with the out of work former members of the working or retired class are forced to depend on credit for the items they need or want. The worst is the elderly, who must try to find a job so they can work until the day they die because the retirement they invested in has been lost.

Money breeding has greatly increased the quantity of money in the world. Today the goods and services available for sale are dwarfed by the quantity of money available to purchase them. Fortunately the money breeders make up a very small portion of the population and have no need for all the goods and services available for sale. In fact, their interest in money has little to do with purchasing goods and services. They have created a whole new use for money—power. In their bastardized use of money, they have totally disrupted the economy. Their manipulations take money out of the hands of the workers that provide the goods and services of the economy. Without their marker, the workers cannot gain access to the goods and services they have earned with their labor. Collection of interest has replaced the business of manufacturing products as the big moneymaker for the wealthy in America. Our economic system has been manipulated to force the working class to borrow the money needed to live their day-to-day lives. More recently the business of collecting interest has been expanded to take advantage of government. Instead of collecting taxes, our government has been manipulated into borrowing the money needed to operate. The rich manipulators now collect interest instead of paying taxes.

CHAPTER 4

MUNICIPAL BONDS

Cities, counties, and states use their tax base to fund massive paychecks for their executives and fund their needs such as improvement or building of schools, roads, bridges, water systems, and other infrastructure projects with funds received by issuing municipal bonds. Bond payments are usually made by homeowners within the municipality through excess tax assessment on their property. Municipal bonds are also issued to pay for new equipment and vehicles needed by the municipality's emergency services and public services.

Municipal bonds are a safe investment for investors because any homeowner who fails to pay his or her share of the principle and interest payments through the assessed property taxes can have his or her house seized and sold to pay the back taxes. The new homeowner, of course, is responsible for paying the continuing assessed taxes.

Reducing the massive salaries of government executives wouldn't entirely negate the need for the issuance of municipal bonds, but it would help. A bigger help would be for government workers to accomplish the needed work instead of paying massive profits to the owners of construction companies so that they can have their employees accomplish the work. Of course, the bonds themselves eat up a sizable portion of taxes collected from the taxpayers in the form of interest on the bonds.

Sensible salaries, responsible administration, and good planning are needed for municipalities to live within the budget allowed by collected taxes. Adding massive executive salaries, profits to campaign contributing business owners, and interest on loans (municipal bonds) to a municipality's expenses, forces excess funds out of the pockets of the hard-working citizens of the municipality.

CHAPTER 5

INSURANCE

The purchase of insurance does not guarantee the purchaser will get anything for his money. The purchaser of an apple gets an apple for his money, but the purchaser of insurance may get nothing more for his money than a piece of paper and peace of mind; neither of which is tangible. Insurance is purchased with money the insured has earned by expending his or her labor to provide a good or a service. The insurance company, in exchange for regular premium payments from the insured's earned income, promises to give the insured nothing. However, the insurance provider may, after the passage of time and in a given instance, purchase a good or a service on behalf of the insured or, if included in the policy, his or her family. Some insurance policies may even specify a specific amount of money to be paid in a given instance.

Most people who buy insurance think they are paying into a pool of money that will be used to help the insured recover from an incident specifically covered by their policy. In fact, the pool of money is used to make investments, and the return on the investments is what is used to pay for claims against the policy.

Lawyers write insurance policy contracts to the benefit of the insurance company because the insurance company wants to keep as much money as possible. Deductibles require the insured to take responsibility for paying for some, and in the case of small claims all, of the covered expense. Automatic rate increases after claims are made is another way the contract discourages the insured from submitting small claims to the insurance company. Claim for a loss can be denied if the insurance company determines the loss occurred under questionable circumstances. The insurance company may pay to cover all the losses for a third party and then force the insured to reimburse it for all expenses because the insurance company determined the insured was at fault. The insured may have what seems to be minor damage to a car he or she has owned since it was new. The insurance company by contract has the right to decide the insured must give up the car and accept a check. The check will be an amount determined by the insurance company to be sufficient to buy a car similar to the one damaged. The deductible will have been withheld from the total prior to issuing the check. The insured, of course, will have to pay the taxes, licensing, and registration as well as the cost withheld for the deductible when purchasing the car previously used by others. In addition, the insured will have to pay higher premiums on the used car to insure it. Insurance contracts give the company the right to decide which medical procedure is best for the insured. The company may also decide the insured should have no medical procedure at all for a given sickness or injury.

I would estimate the average working person pays monthly premiums on no less than five insurance policies and quite possibly more. For most people, the total dollar amount paid for premiums on these policies far exceeds the total claims ever made. This means the insured has taken his or her right to goods and services within the economy earned by his or her labor used to produce a like amount of goods or services and given those rights away for, in most cases, nothing.

The insurance company invests the premiums paid by the insured. The investment may be a temporary or long-term injection of money into the economy for a return with interest, or it may be an investment in stocks or bonds. No matter what the investment, it is made with funds the investor did not earn through the fruit of his or her labor that will return money the investor did not earn with the fruit of his or her labor. They are simply breeding money.

The insurance companies have little or no need of a large infrastructure to support their operations, so their income from all sources minus their operating cost plus outlays for claims should leave them with an enormous tax bill. The insurance companies, of course, want to keep their money, so they increase their expenditures with massive salaries for their top echelons and fairly decent commissions for their agents. They have massive office buildings built and furnish the offices with extravagant décor to house their investment personnel, lawyers, management executives, and advertising specialists. Private jets are kept at various locations about the country for transport of key personnel. Plush recreational estates are purchased and maintained for meetings as well as entertainment. To the greatest extent possible, every bit of income that might create tax liability is invested in some way to avoid the payment of taxes.

CHAPTER 6

GOVERNMENT SUBSIDIES

Government subsidy is simply lip service to consumer savings because the money the consumer saves at the marketplace is taken away in the form of taxes to pay the subsidy.

Subsidies give unfair advantage when businesses that sell like items are in competition, and one business is given a subsidy, and the other is not. The subsidized business is able to sell its product at a lower price than the unsubsidized business. The unsubsidized business may find no market for its product at the unsubsidized price, in which case the unsubsidized business will be forced out of business.

The consumer seldom directly purchases subsidized items. Take for instance the subsidy paid to tomato growers. The subsidies go to growers that produce a massive crop. These crops are predominantly sold to customers in the business of manufacturing goods such as pizza sauce, catsup, or tomato sauce. Smaller farms don't qualify for the subsidy because the farmer doesn't grow enough tomatoes.

Corn is another crop that is highly subsidized and never purchased by individuals because the subsidized corn isn't edible. The taste is dreadful, the texture is tough, and the nutritional value is nonexistent. The entire yield of all of the subsidized corn is purchased by businesses. The largest portion of the corn is processed into high fructose corn syrup, which is used in the manufacture of almost every processed food found in the grocery store. The byproducts of the process that makes the high fructose corn syrup make their way into many other manufactured products such as animal feed, corn syrup, and even fuel.

Milk is a highly publicized subsidized product, but the majority of the subsidized milk is sold to manufactures that process it into cheese. The subsidy increases the profits of the cheese producers as well as the big four pizza companies. The small dairy farms that are not big enough to qualify for the subsidies are disappearing.

The small farmers that grow the variety of crops our bodies need to be healthy are being forced off their land by the big growers of the four genetically engineered crops our government subsidizes: wheat, corn, soybeans, and rice. The genetically engineered crops are not as wholesome as their ancestors, but they produce many more bushels per acre and are easier to grow. Thanks to government subsidies, the massive yield can be sold to manufacturers at low prices so that the profits of the manufacturers can be maximized. The result is that the food available for consumption, although filled with calories, is low in nutrition, while the food that is high in nutrition and low in calories is increasing in price and dropping in availability.

Government subsidies do not stop with food. Our railroads are subsidized to the point they need not upgrade their equipment to the point where they could provide the valuable, time-saving, safe, fuel-efficient service of transporting the public. Instead they use their antiquated equipment to bilk subsidies from the taxpayers. Of course, the elected officials who accept railroad dollars for their election campaigns assure us the subsidies are needed so the railroads will stay in business to provide their limited service, which seems to be awfully important, to the elected officials at least.

The airlines, which would be severely impacted by an unsubsidized properly run railroad, are also subsidized directly as well as indirectly.

I could go on, but I think you get the point. Subsidies are made for the benefit of the subsidized not the taxpayer. In fact, more often than not government subsidies paid with our tax dollars adversely affect the taxpayer.

CHAPTER 7

DERIVATIVES

A derivative is a contract or security that derives its value from an item specifically named in the contract or security. The item named can be a commodity such as green beans, pork bellies, fuel, or gold. The item could also be another security, or the value of a rate such as interest or currency exchange, or an index of asset value such as a stock index. Insurance policies are derivatives. The bundles of loans discussed in the chapter "Breeding Money" are derivatives.

Our free market (free of government regulation) has created an opportunity for Big banks and investors to use derivatives to extract large sums of money from businesses with which they otherwise have nothing to do. The consumer who buys the products of the business is charged an artificially inflated price, which includes the cost of the product as well as the cost of the extracted funds.

Many Americans see the fluctuating, ridiculously high, cost of gasoline and think it is attributable to the greedy gas companies. In truth, a large portion of the price as well as most of the fluctuation in price is due to derivatives. Speculators who have nothing at all to do with the production, distribution, or sale of gasoline drastically increase the price by buying and selling crude oil and gasoline derivatives, more commonly known as commodities.

Diesel fuel used to be sold for a price cheaper than regular gasoline but now is priced higher than supreme gasoline. Diesel is still cheaper to produce than gasoline but speculators using derivatives are able to extract large sums of money from the economy by buying and selling diesel based derivatives because trucks, which are mostly fueled by diesel, move everything for sale. The increased cost of transportation caused by the speculated increase in Diesel prices is included in the price of every product sold. Fuels are relatively latecomers in the derivatives market but the increasing cost of gasoline has gained significant American attention.

The first use of derivatives, thousands of years ago, was for food. Today derivatives are still being used in food production and recently have managed to starve millions of people in Third World countries because these people can't afford the artificially inflated cost of food. Derivatives didn't come into being to increase prices but rather to protect farmers and stabilize prices. A contract (derivative) is made between someone with a lot of money to spare and a farmer. The financier buys a farmer's crop at a fair price per bushel on the expected yield before the crop is planted. The sale gives the farmer money to plant the crop and support his family for the year. If the yield is less than expected or the price per bushel drops, the investor, who is in a better position to afford the loss, absorbs the loss. The investor's hope, of course, is that the total value of the harvested crop will be higher than the price paid for the crop.

Deregulation of the banks has made credit far more profitable than producing a product for sale. Those who extract money from the economy through collection of interest must find new ways to invest their fortunes. Derivatives are becoming a very popular investment. Investors buy and sell product-based derivatives many times before the consumer has an opportunity to buy the product. The difference between the original price of a product and the derived price goes to the investors. In other words, the consumer is paying a profit to people who have nothing to do with the production or distribution of the product they are buying.

One of the more visible, if not obvious, derivatives in wide use is insurance. Medical insurance has proven to be detrimental to health— mental, physical, and financial. Homeowner's insurance may pay for the loss of the insured's house, but it also may not if the cause of the loss was not foreseen and specifically covered in the policy.

Not all insurance derivatives are obvious to the insurer. If this happens, I'll pay you; as long as it doesn't happen, you pay me, are the basic terms of many multimillion-dollar derivatives. The guarantor in many cases is a group of retirement accounts (IRAs and 401s). As long as whatever is named in the terms of the derivative doesn't happen, the administrator of the retirement accounts gets a regular payment. A small portion of the payment goes to each of the individual accounts. The regular payments are a blessing to the workers looking forward to retirement. If whatever is named in the terms of the derivative does happen, then the money to make up for whatever happened comes from the retirement accounts. The multimillion-dollar loss could instantly empty all the retirement accounts associated with the derivative.

Some banks use derivatives to make more of their depositor's funds available for loans. The bank is supposed to be responsible with the money it loans because if that money is not paid back, then they have lost the investment they have made with the depositor's money. But if they can get someone else to say, "I will accept the risk," then the bank can loan out more of the depositor's money. The bank, by contract (derivative), agrees to pay the party assuming the risk a regular payment for the service.

CHAPTER 8

TAX DEDUCTIONS

There is a limit to the quantity of goods or services a single person can provide, so the higher his or her income, the more likely it is that a substantial portion of that income doesn't equate directly to the goods or services the person provided to get that income. In fact, many of the people who provide no good or service make the highest incomes. Tax deductions allow those that take the most money out of the economy and place the least goods or services into the economy to pay, by percentage of income, the lowest taxes.

CHAPTER 9

PERSONAL INCOME

Business managers regularly allocate the goods and services their employees are entitled to through the expenditure of their labor to themselves or to the business they manage. Consequently the workers have to severely budget their spending in order to make it from paycheck to paycheck. Many workers are not successful in their efforts and incur debt that must be paid with subsequent paychecks, which makes it even more difficult to financially make it from one payday to the next.

The number of people with no income is growing daily. Most of them wish to work but can find no job. The competition for jobs is what makes it possible for employers to take, for themselves or the business they manage, the goods and services their employees are entitled to through the expenditure of their labor.

The out of work, of course, contribute nothing to consumer spending while the contributions to consumer spending by workers shrinks with their income. Consumer spending fuels the economy. The reduction of consumer spending contributes to further loss of jobs and perpetuates the downward spiral of the economy. In order for the economy to thrive, every worker needs to have a job that pays a living wage, which includes cash left over for extras as well as savings.

CHAPTER 10

UNEMPLOYMENT

Unemployment is a planned fact of our economy. Businesses, large and small, strongly desire a portion of the population to be unemployed. Unemployment keeps wages and salaries low. The employed end up living paycheck to paycheck and seldom have enough money to pay for all their needs, which generally leaves nothing for their wants and desires.

Unemployment means cheap labor for business, but it means homelessness and hunger, possibly starvation, for the unemployed. Unemployment Insurance is available to those who have recently worked and paid a percentage of their income into the state's unemployment insurance account. The unemployment insurance payments are less than the pay a worker received before becoming unemployed, which means the unemployed worker has even less money with which to pay his or her overwhelming bills. Any attempt the unemployed worker makes, through temporary part-time employment, to make up for some of his or her lost income is met with the penalty of a reduced unemployment payment.

Unemployment is detrimental to the economy because it reduces the number of consumers available to purchase the products of business. Another factor that affects business is the amount of disposable income available to those who have a job. It's ironic that business owners are so fixated on their bottom line that they are oblivious to the fact that they collectively are partially responsible for the failure of their business.

CHAPTER 11

A HOUSE

Owning a house is a desire held by most Americans. To satisfy this desire, there needs to be enough extra income on each paycheck for a worker to save enough money to purchase a house within a reasonable amount of time. What is reasonable? It took my grandfather, a factory worker, five years to save the money needed to purchase his house. I would say that is reasonable. The house was purchased around 1920 and cost in the neighborhood of $5,000. The same house could have been sold for $1 million in 2005 if my aunt, who still lived in the house, had chosen to sell it.

I purchased my first house in 1978 for $27,000. It was customary at that time to put down 10 percent of the house's value as a down payment and then finance the remainder for a period of thirty years. I was able to purchase my house with a veteran's loan so I didn't need a down payment. I made house payments for fifteen years before selling the house. My final check from the sale was $7,000. After fifteen years of payments I had only paid off $4,000 of the principle, but I had already paid much more than $27,000 in interest. I would say that paying the seller's price in full with a loan and then paying the bank much more than the seller price in interest was unreasonable, but in my children's time, things are much worse.

My niece wanted to buy a house, so she and her husband started to save for a down payment. They figured $10,000 would be sufficient, but, of course, while they were saving, the price of houses continued to rise. To their benefit, or should we say their detriment, they were finally able to buy a house when banking practice was changed to eliminate the need for a down payment. Their purchase price was over $400,000 and the terms were interest only, subprime, variable interest. This gave them an initial payment they could afford. The "interest only" meant they would be paying nothing on the principle, a concept they didn't quite understand. The "subprime"/"variable interest" meant their payments would at least rise to the prime rate. Like many first-time homebuyers, neither my niece nor her husband understood at the time of the sale that their house payment would increase over time, and, of course, the payment didn't cease to increase once it reached the prime interest rate.

My niece was lucky because the market price of her house continued to rise for a time after the sale. By the time the house payment reached a level they could no longer afford, they had sufficient equity in the house to qualify for refinancing. The new terms have a fixed interest rate and include payments on the principle. Since the refinance, the housing market has begun to decline, and the market value of the house is less than they owe, but at least they can afford the payments, and there will come a day when the house is finally paid off. Other buyers have not been so lucky.

CHAPTER 12

CREDIT

The average working-class paycheck barely pays for the necessities of raising a family. To acquire desired items and oftentimes even some necessities, many people resort to using credit. Credit is so easy to get that many people don't satisfy themselves with a few of their wants. They buy everything they want. The payments on the balance of their credit purchases together with the accompanying interest often takes up so much of their meager paycheck that they are forced to use credit to purchase more of their necessities.

Consumer credit is a trap. The more you use it, the more you need it. It wouldn't be so bad if the credit was given without interest as the Bible declares it should be. Many who get the credit become needy long before it is paid off. The creditors not only don't eliminate the interest when it becomes a serious financial problem, but rather increase it and then add penalties when the payments are late.

Even without interest on borrowed money, it is too easy to overextend oneself when the money being spent has not yet been earned. Credit should be reserved for those who use the money for manufacturing a product—. accepting, of course, that the manufactured product has greater value than the sum of the raw materials to make it, the total processing cost, and the interest. Any other use of credit has detrimental effects to an economy, which may be hidden in the short term but will most certainly be seen in the long run.

In the early twenty-first century, some are singing the praises of credit while others are shouting warnings. It should be obvious that no one, whether an individual, a country, or any entity in between, can continue barrowing indefinitely. The ones singing praises may think the escalating loan balances will someday be miraculously paid. This, of course, can only happen if income is suddenly and dramatically increased.

CHAPTER 13

BUSINESS

Business schools teach their students that "the purpose of a business is to make a profit." It's quite often argued by new, unsuspecting students that the purpose of a business should be to make a product. The instructor is very quick to make the questioning student look like an idiot. Once the student is completely cowered, the instructor will grant that a business has to make a product or perform a service in order to make a profit.

The problem with the current curriculum taught is that it creates a mind-set in our business owners that leads to poor working conditions, low pay, poor quality products, ridiculously high prices, lousy service, inhumane business decisions as well as downright bad business decisions, and potential customers who don't make enough money and/or keep enough money after interest, insurance, and taxes are paid to afford the business's product. The mentality leaves no room for caring about employees, the quality of a product, the completeness of a service, or the good of the community, much less benefits to the country.

Employees are regularly laid off during slow times so a business can preserve profits. It doesn't matter in the least that the employee is depending on his or her income to support a family and that the business would not be hurt by reduced profits. The doctrine "the purpose of a business is to make a profit" is held close and so ingrained that the well-being of the employee is of no concern to business managers. Ironically, the businesses that lay off workers don't realize their businesses are being hurt by the reduction in consumer spending brought about by the layoffs.

Products are made as cheaply as possible so that profits can be maximized. The quality of the product is of secondary importance at best. Customers would prefer a product to last as long as possible, but the manufacturer, looking to maximize profits, wants the product to break, the sooner the better, so that the customer will buy a new product sooner. The technology market has gone one step further by ensuring that the newest products become obsolete within a couple years after manufacture. They further ensure the retirement of the fairly new products by ensuring incompatibility with newer products.

I submit that our young business students should be taught that the purpose of a business is to manufacture a product or provide a service. The business should manufacture the highest quality product it is capable of producing and/or provide the best service the business is capable of providing. Giving the customer the best product and/or service the business is able to provide will encourage the customer to come back and, in addition, tell his or her friends about the business. Incidentally, in order to stay in business the business must make a profit. Furthermore, it should be impressed on our prospective entrepreneurs that happy, loyal employees pass on their happiness to customers, promoting repeat business and increased profits. Developing this type of mentality would be good for our nation's communities as well as the country as a whole, and it wouldn't do the business any harm either.

Strong, healthy businesses make for a stronger country. Exporting business and thereby jobs weakens a country and will eventually result in its fall.

CHAPTER 14

FROM ROBBER BARONS TO INTEREST BARONS

The robber barons of the nineteenth century built America's wealth through industry. Although the process required massive manpower expenditures, the captains of industry felt they should be the only ones to profit from America's good fortune. Laborers were at work in the mills before the sun came up and labored until after the sun went down for pennies a day. Worker benefits from factory owners were nonexistent. If a worker could no longer work due to injury incurred on the job, he was out of work, no compensation paid. A sick worker came to work or lost his job.

Labor finally organized itself into unions and collectively fought for better working conditions and higher pay. The struggle was long and hard, and the goal was slowly achieved. The unions were not satisfied with their hard-won prize. They continued their fight and forced the formation of benefits for the workers; sick pay, worker compensation for injury, even vacation pay, was eventually seen by the workers. The labor unions became a force to be reckoned with. They continued demanding raises and increased benefits until the owners of industry finally gave up and moved their operations outside the United States, where labor was cheaper and more easily exploited.

Americans with money, who didn't want to invest overseas, were forced to find a business that needed little or no manpower to turn a profit.

Loaning money at interest was a natural choice. The groundwork was laid by using the control over the government, which substantial campaign contributions had provided. Legislation was quickly enacted to facilitate loans for construction and purchase of housing.

Building houses employed the labor that no longer had a factory in which to work. The transition was so smooth that America hardly noticed the loss of its industry. Developers borrowed money to buy land, purchase building material, and employ labor. New homeowners borrowed money to purchase the newly erected houses. Qualified buyers emptied their saving accounts for a down payment and filled the new houses. Eventually it became obvious that there would soon be more houses than buyers.

New legislation in the form of deregulation was the answer. It wasn't hard to sell our elected officials as well as the public with the notion that it is the right of every American to own a house. The money continued to flow, and the need for a down payment became a thing of the past. Housing prices rose so quickly that unqualified buyers could sell or refinance their houses to make up for their financial shortages.

The interest collecting business was doing so well with housing that it was only natural to expand the market. Credit cards became the next big moneymaker for the rich. The working class was spending so much of their income on housing, most of which was interest, that they didn't have enough money left over to buy the things they wanted. Credit cards opened the door to unlimited spending. The out-of-control balances on credit cards were dealt with by refinancing home loans on the houses, which were rapidly increasing in value.

The interest barons, using their immense control over our government, forced the introduction of legislation to provide themselves with even more tax breaks than they had previously arranged. They used their influence to convince our elected officials that borrowing was the answer to the country's monetary shortfalls. Their methods were nothing less than brilliant. Instead of paying taxes, the rich loan our government operating capital and then collect interest on their investment.

CHAPTER 15

WHERE DOES THE MONEY GO?

Whether you make $25,000 a year or $250,000 a year, by the end of the year most people wonder, "Where did the money go?" No matter how much money you make, it all seems to just disappear.

The 3 percent of America's population that controls our government through their campaign contributions spends so little of their annual income on living expenses that it is hardly noticeable to them. That's not to say the figure is small. In fact, the dollar amount spent on living expenses would probably bankrupt most of the remaining 97 percent of the population. In addition to having living expenses that make up only a small percentage of their annual income, the wealthiest American's, who make up only 3 percent of the population and have most of America's money, need not pay for insurance because they have sufficient funds available to pay for any mishap or health-related difficulty. Interest, a major expense for 97 percent of the population, is of no consequence to the remaining 3 percent. The only time this group borrows money is when they need extra funds for an investment that will make them more money.

Ninety-seven percent of America's population loses more than half of their income to interest, insurance, and taxes. The remainder of their income is spent on living expenses. The majority of the 97 percent run out of money before they pay for these four categories of mandatory expenditures and end up borrowing to pay for the remainder of their needs as well as any wants they feel they can allow themselves.

Insurance payments are a major monthly expenditure for the majority of Americans. In Washington State, as well as other states, it has become mandatory for everyone who drives a car to have automobile insurance. (Guess who lobbied for that law!) Most years this expenditure buys nothing for the person forced to pay the bill, and when there is a need, the insurance company may very well find an excuse not to pay for damages. The insured, however, is almost certain to pay for a portion if not all the damages.

Medical insurance generally costs a great deal more than the ridiculously high premiums charged monthly by the auto insurance companies. In addition to the monthly premiums for medical insurance, the insured generally pays deductibles and/or copays for any medical treatment, the cost of which usually exceeds the entire cost of what the medical treatment would have cost before the advent of medical insurance. The medical insurance companies have even more ways of avoiding payment on behalf of the insured than the automobile insurance companies. It is quite common for the medical insurance companies to stall a person in need of life-saving medical treatment until the person dies, thus saving the insurance company from all the medical cost that would have ensued in keeping the patient alive.

Medical insurance is regularly denied to those who have a great likelihood of needing medical care. The federal government tried to reform medical insurance to make it fairer for the insured. Eliminating the right of the insurance company to refuse coverage for preexisting conditions was one of the changes proposed and possibly the only good thing to come out of the effort. After the original bill was introduced, the insurance companies used their immense wealth to influence the content of the bill. The two biggest changes now are an increase in insurance rates and the requirement that all Americans pay for medical insurance. In preparation of enacting the new law, many insurance companies have increased patient deductibles, and many more are increasing their rates.

Very few homeowners can afford to purchase their home in cash. One of the requirements of getting a loan to buy a home is the homeowner must carry insurance on the home. House insurance generally covers fire and theft. Additional flood insurance is required if the home is located on a flood plain. Flood insurance, which usually costs more than basic home insurance, covers little or nothing. Flood insurance is controlled by FEMA, a federal government agency. Big money through lobbying and campaign contributions has managed to arrange for all assessment of damage, needed repair to correct the damage, and the repair work for flood damage be done by government contract; the contract is held by one major nationwide corporation.

The theft portion of homeowners' insurance has limits to its coverage on selected items. Most homeowners find out about these limits after they have a loss. The insurance company refuses to cover the full cost of the loss, increases the premiums because of the claim, and then gets to add riders to the policy by convincing the homeowner that the purchase of the riders will assure that any future losses will be covered in full.

Life insurance is very important to 97 percent of the population because the loss of a breadwinner can leave the family in financial ruin. The average cost of a funeral is more than most families can afford. The life insurance must be sufficient to pay for the funeral, as well as make up for the lost income. If there is more than one breadwinner in the household, then the insurance has to pay off enough debt to allow the remaining breadwinner to continue on with the payments for the remaining bills. If there is only one breadwinner, then the insurance must be enough to pay off all of the debt and leave enough money left over to live on until a new source of income can be established.

Insurance may seem to be a good way to protect your investment, but you have to ask yourself, "Does the cost of premiums offset the potential loss?" It's not like the insurance prevents bad things from happening, and when or if they do, there is no guarantee the insurance company will reimburse you for your loss or pay for your needs resulting from injury or poor health. Insurance may just be a major monthly expense, perpetrated on 97 percent of the population by the wealthy 3 percent, that has no true value.

Prior to 1920, buying a house in cash was the norm; today very few of our population can afford to pay cash for a house. A very small portion of a monthly house payment goes toward paying for the house. The majority of each house payment is accrued interest, and this interest accounts for, on the average, 35 percent of the total household income.

Cars are another major purchase that used to be done with cash. Car loans are available from banks and credit unions, but many people chose to let the car dealer take care of the financing for them. No matter what the source, car loans, including their associated interest, take up a large portion of a family's monthly income.

The average American's monthly income is reduced by interest paid toward the balance owed on credit cards. These balances generally increase each month rather than decrease because there is insufficient income to pay for all the family needs, resulting in only the minimum credit card payments being made while more charges are added to the cards.

Those Americans that make less than $250,000 a year generally pay a higher percentage of their income to income tax. That's not because their income is in a higher tax bracket. In fact, the opposite is true. The reason they pay a higher percentage of their income is because they do not make enough money to take advantage of all the tax breaks available to those with a higher income.

Everyone who makes less than $115,000 a year pays 7.5 percent of his or her income to Social Security. All income above $115,000 is exempt from the tax. Therefore, everyone who makes more than $115,000 a year pays a smaller percentage of their income to Social Security and is guaranteed to receive the maximum benefit allowed.

Homeowners are assessed taxes on their home every year. This tax is often collected with the regular house payment and then paid by the mortgage company when due. Those who do not pay the tax in this way receive a bill for their taxes. Those who rent pay the taxes for their landlord as part of their rent.

Paying the taxes and licensing fees for a new car purchase adds significantly to the debt of buying a new car. The charges don't stop there.

Every year the car owner gets to pay again for licensing and, in most states, taxes.

In most states, everything you buy is taxed. This is a sore subject for most, so let's look at the bright side. If half your income goes to interest, insurance, and taxes, then that means half your income is free of sales tax. Or is it? Most working people today use credit to make the needed purchases their reduced income will not cover.

Check what you pay annually for all the aforementioned taxes, insurance, and interest. You will probably find that it already accounts for 50 percent of your income, but as I stated at the beginning, most of us pay more than 50 percent of our income to interest, insurance, and taxes. The price of gasoline has a great deal of taxes included. Taxes on your phone can easily add up to the cost of your basic phone. This means if you have a home phone with no extras and no long distance, then half your bill goes to taxes. Do you have cable? Look at your bill. You might be surprised to see how much of your charge is added taxes.

Now that we have looked at how much of our pay goes to interest, insurance, and taxes, three expenses we have nothing to show for, let's see where the rest of our paycheck disappears.

Housing, something almost everyone who earns $25,000 or more a year has, costs on the average 40 percent of our income for all but the 3 percent who possess most of the money. About 85 percent of your house payment is interest. For those who rent, the figure may be a little smaller because what you pay for rent has been increased to allow for your landlord's profit. Ten percent of the remaining 15 percent accounts for taxes and insurance; the last 5 percent is principle. So you can say that housing costs only 5 percent of your income, the rest already being accounted for under interest, insurance, and taxes. For those who rent an apartment from one of the massive corporations that own their property outright, there is no interest and quite possibly no insurance or taxes paid out of your rent. In your case, the 40 percent of your income paid to rent is all tribute to the 3 percent of the population that controls most of the money.

Car payments are one monthly payment from which many people never get free. For some, it is because they buy a new car and then trade it in for another new car before or shortly after it is paid for. For others, who can't afford a new car, their used car wears out soon after the last payment is made, if not before. The car you drive is generally quite dependent on your income. It is not uncommon for the cost of driving a car to take up 15 to 20 percent of the household income; of course, a large percentage of that monthly expense is interest, insurance, and taxes, so let's attribute 10 percent of our income to car payments.

Although the daily calories a person needs to subsist are not influenced by income, the amount of money spent to acquire those calories may vary greatly with income. A person with a higher income, for instance, may decide to have more meals outside the home. Another variance may be in the choice of food. A healthy diet, high in fresh lean meat, fruits, and vegetables, is going to cost more than an unhealthy diet high in fats and carbohydrates.

In many households, home phones are giving way to cell phones. The primary reason may be the inability to pay for both or simply the desire to use the saved money elsewhere. Cable TV is another expense shared by most households, especially since the loss of analog service. Telephone and cable, while common in most households, are elective; utilities are not. If you have a place of residence, you must have utilities. Some may argue that they can get by without them, but in most areas of the country it is a law that you must have them. (Guess who lobbied to pass that law?)

By now, for many people, I have probably answered the question, "Where does all the money go?" because by the time they get to that point in the month where all the above mentioned bills are paid, many people have run out of money and are pulling their credit cards out of their wallet instead of cash. The credit card bills were not mentioned above except where they were associated with their interest, but that is probably okay because the portion of the credit card bill that accounts for the principle is probably only 2 to 3 percent of the balance.

Some, the more financially well off or the more frugal of the 97 percent of our population we have been referring to, still have funds available from the monthly income. This is good because we still have not talked about clothes, which are not usually an every month expense; gas, which is; car repairs, which hopefully are not; and all the wants that every member of the family has.

Each year, a majority of the 97 percent of our country's population goes deeper into debt to pay for their needs and some wants because they are forced to pay more than half their income to insurance, interest, and taxes. The wealthiest people, who make up the other 3 percent, need expend none of their income on interest or insurance and pay little or no tax on their massive income because they have so much control over our government that they are able to influence the formation of our extremely complicated tax laws. Our tax laws fill volumes. They are not made complicated in order to cover every eventuality of business and thereby collect every possible penny from the rich but rather to allow the rich sufficient maneuverability to avoid paying taxes.

CHAPTER 16

THE STOCK MARKET

The stock market is an invaluable economic tool. Some consumer commodities can't make it from the mind of the inventor to a viable consumer commodity without the expenditure of more money than the inventor can borrow from a bank. The travel service industries likewise wouldn't be possible without the stock market. What bank could loan a business enough money to buy a jet, much less a whole fleet of jets? Someone might have enough money or be able to borrow enough money to buy a train engine, but what about the whole train or the tracks on which the train runs?

The stock market is a good place for those with adequate savings to place excess cash for an investment on which they can expect a later return. Of course, there is no guarantee of a later return or a return at all. In fact, the entire investment could be lost if the inventor's great idea produces a commodity the consumer doesn't wish to purchase. The possibility of a loss is why it makes sense to only invest cash that the investor can afford to lose.

The stockholder benefits most when he or she owns stock in a domestic corporation that manufactures a product. The premise is that the manufacturing process is of such a large scale that the money can't be borrowed from a bank to finance the entire operation. That being true, the stockholder is part owner in a massive building and possibly multiple buildings, specialized machinery to accomplish the manufacturing process, and the raw materials needed to make the finished products of the business.

The stockholders benefit each time the manufacturing process on a unit of product is completed because of the difference between the value of the finished product and the cost of the raw materials together with the cost of the manufacturing process. The increase in stock value and the dividends paid as a result of the profits on the sale of the finished products are also benefits to the stockholder.

The laborers that built the finished product spend their income, which contributes to national consumer spending. This contributes to the continuation of the operation of the nation's economy, a benefit to the nation as a whole, of which the stockholder is a part.

The raw materials are in many cases finished products of another manufacturer. The raw material contributing manufacturer's employees contribute to national consumer spending, but they also, as does the stockholders corporation's employees, pay tax from their income, which helps the government operate.

Income taxes are not the only taxes collected from the operation of the corporation and its suppliers. There are taxes on property, sales taxes, transportation taxes, and more. The benefits to the stockholder from the collected taxes are not as direst as the collected dividends or the increased price the stock can be sold for, but there are derived benefits.

During the early portion of the twenty-first century, the nation has learned the benefit of consumer spending and filled government coffers through the collection of taxes by seeing what happens when there is a lack of both. There is one more benefit to the stockholders of a domestic manufacturing corporation and the nation as a whole. The benefit is more direct and, if you think about it, obvious.

The products the corporation manufactures are available for purchase. What good is it to have money if there is nothing to buy? The stockholders of medical insurance corporations, for example, make lots of money, but their corporation contributes nothing tangible to the stockholders or the nation. What they do contribute is an increased cost of medical care for the sick and injured. Part of this increased cost goes to pay for the massive salaries paid to corporate executives, the massive office buildings they inhabit, and the private jets corporate officers use for their transportation.

The contributions of retail corporations are questionable. Granted they buy a product at a price, place it on their shelves for a higher price, and then pay their stockholders a dividend from their profits. So they meet the expectancy of their investors and even contribute in a small way to taxes, but overall they are a detriment. All that is needed for a retailer to go into business is a building large enough to hold merchandise and the merchandise. Banks can loan the money needed if a would-be entrepreneur doesn't have enough money of his or her own. In times past, the best retailers, the ones that gave the most caring service and in most cases understood their products enough to inform their customers about the products, were the small retailers that lived upstairs of the store. The large corporate stores, which don't seem to care about their customers or their employees, and which generally know nothing of the products on the shelves, have for the most part run these small, caring retailers out of business.

Manufacturing of large products such as planes, trains, and automobiles can only be accomplished by corporate investment—likewise, many other commodities. However, not all manufacturing requires corporate investment; wherever possible, manufacturing should be done on a smaller scale because more care can be given to the quality of the product. Graduating taxes are the equalizer that makes it possible for small manufacturers to compete with large manufacturers. However, the corporate stranglehold on our elected officials has all but eliminated corporate taxes.

In order to facilitate the manufacture of some products, stocks need to be sold, and corporations need to be formed. The sale of any stock, including manufacturing, should be looked at carefully, and the decision in most cases should be made to not allow the formation of the corporation. Legislation of hard, fast rules is not the answer. First of all, laws can be circumvented, but, more importantly, there are potentially beneficial corporations that don't manufacture a product and equally beneficial corporations that manufacture a high-quality small product in great numbers. A vast reduction of the stock market, of course, would destroy the concept of using the stock market to fund everyone's retirement, but as you will see before the end of this section, the practice of trying to fund everyone's retirement with the stock market has already set up the destruction of the stock market.

The value of the total assets of a corporation minus the corporation's liabilities is equal to how much the corporation is actually worth to the stockholders or, in other words, the stockholders equity. Dividing the stockholders' equity by the total shares of stock outstanding gives the book value of each outstanding share of stock.

The market value of each stock is, very simply, the price the stock is selling for.

These figures would seem to be the same, but they seldom are because anyone that knows the true value of the total assets of a corporation or its total liabilities, by law, is not allowed to buy or sell the stock. To do so is called trading with inside information.

A manufacturing corporation's stock is probably the easiest example to follow for understanding stock value. There are obvious assets owned by a manufacturing corporation. The building or buildings they do their manufacturing in is one. The machinery used to manufacture their product is another. Some corporate manufacturers have warehouses, separate from their factory, in which they store their raw materials, which will eventually be used in the manufacturing process. They may also have warehouses in which they store their finished products that are waiting to be shipped to the buyer. The raw materials and finished goods, as well as the building in which they are stored, are assets of the corporation. There are also assets that are not so obvious.

Manufacturing corporations, by their nature, have a lot of income. The income is generally not used right away, so it must be stored. A bank may be the obvious choice for storing money, but banks pay very low interest on deposited money. Inflation often can make money sitting in a bank account for an extended period of time lose value. The advantage of a bank account is that the money is readily available for use in paying liabilities or making cash purchases, so corporations do keep a certain amount of their funds in a bank to cover operating expenses. Stocks and bonds usually pay a better rate of return than a bank, so the majority of a corporation's cash assets are invested. Bonds pay interest to the owner, and some stocks pay dividends. The income from the interest and dividends is constantly being reinvested in more stocks and bonds, but it can also be placed in a bank account or spent on an expansion of the corporation, so ownership of stocks and bonds in other corporations can be assets adding to the book value of a manufacturing corporation's stock.

The liabilities of a manufacturing corporation are the cost of raw materials, the utilities used but not yet paid for, labor expended before payday, and any debts incurred, along with accompanying accrued interest, such as a mortgage taken out for a needed renovation on a factory building or a debt on new equipment—basically any money the corporation owes.

Most of the assets of a manufacturing corporation are tangible and contribute directly to its income. Even its liabilities, such as raw materials and new equipment bought on credit, contribute to its income.

Retail corporations are very similar in that they have concrete assets and some liabilities that result in a profit. One way in which they differ is that any retail corporation can be replaced by a non-corporate entity or entities with limited resources, whereas some manufacturing processes can only be accomplished through the use of vast recourses, which can only be accumulated by the formation of a large corporation.

Insurance corporations are a different animal altogether. They have no tangible moneymaking assets. They accept money from their clients in return for a contract that might entitle the client to a later cash payment or help with some unforeseen expense. Insurance corporations sell stock so they can purchase needed working facilities, hire personnel, pay for start-up supplies and equipment such as office furniture, computers, printed forms, and more. In addition, they use the invested funds to pay off any claims that arise before they have accrued sufficient funds to pay for the claims.

The real business of insurance corporations is investing. They invest client premiums in various stocks and bonds and then gamble that they will get a high enough return on their investments to pay off claims (liabilities) and thereby increase owner's equity. The stockholders of insurance corporation stock are indirectly nothing more than group-stockholders of many varied stocks and bonds.

The tangible assets of insurance corporations are their office buildings, office furniture, office supplies, and equipment, and for some insurance corporations their fleets of cars, private jets, and recreation property. None of the tangible assets directly contribute to corporate income. Corporate income is derived from premiums paid for insurance, dividends from stocks, and interest on bonds. There is also a net increase in corporate worth from the appreciation in value of stocks they hold in other corporations.

The liabilities of insurance corporations are the claims made by their clients, accumulated salaries not yet paid to their executives, accumulated wages not yet paid to their workers, earned commissions not yet paid to their agents, utilities for their office buildings, and all the accounts payable for their office supplies and other operating expenses, such as jet fuel.

The stockholder's equity in an insurance corporation amounts to the value of all the corporation's stocks and bond holdings plus the non-income producing tangible assets minus its liabilities.

The stock market is nothing more than a form of financing. It offers an opportunity for investment to those with money to spare. The invested money not only offers a possible financial gain to the investor but also the opportunity to help a potentially beneficial business come into existence.

The stock market can also be used to help a not so beneficial business come into existence. Let's look at what might happen if a theoretical retailer sold stock to launch a chain of massive stores. To keep merchandise close at hand, let's say this retailer builds warehouses throughout the United States. With large warehouses central to a number of stores, the corporation can purchase commodities for resale by the truckload and have them brought to the warehouses. Since our retailer has so much money available from its investors, let's say it purchases a fleet of trucks and trailers to move its product from its warehouses to its stores.

The purchasing power of such a large corporation would give it the ability to demand the lowest price possible on products. Of course, the sheer volume of its need would preclude the corporation from doing business with small manufacturers.

What if this retailer decided to go into direct competition with a well-established large retail chain? In their effort to compete, they build their new stores in close proximity to the targeted stores. The strategy makes good sense because a proven customer base is already established. The new retailer's private warehouses, which gave it the ability to control prices, give it an edge against its competitor. In fact, the new retailer may use its control over the large manufacturing companies to demand its competitor's cost of products increases.

What if this new retailer noticed that not only was it effective at bankrupting its intended target but the small privately owned stores in the area where its new stores were being built started to falter and eventually go into bankruptcy? As a result, it may expand its line and try to purposefully run more stores out of business so that it might enjoy an even larger market share of the retail business.

The success might encourage even more investors to invest, and the retail corporation might be able to buy its own ships. With its own ships, it could purchase the cheapest products to be found anywhere in the world. The retail corporation could buy these foreign-made products by the container load and thereby reduce the price it pays for its products below the previous low prices it demanded from domestic businesses.

Using the stock market to finance this retail enterprise makes good financial sense for the investors and great business sense for the retailer. However, it is economically devastating for the country and its people in general. Thousands of retail businesses are forced to close their doors and go into bankruptcy. The employees of all these businesses as well as the business owners have lost their jobs. Some may have found employment at the new retailer, but you can rest assured their rate of pay is less because the new retailer has fewer businesses to compete with for employees. Many small privately owned manufacturers lose their customer base and go out of business. Their employees as well as the business owners are out of work and probably have little or no prospect of finding another job. Because the manufacturing jobs have moved overseas, which leads to a downturn in the economy, even with retraining the job prospects of the displaced workers and owners are dim. Larger domestic manufacturers and retailers are likely slowly following in the footsteps of the small privately owned manufacturers and retailers; many more lost jobs. All the lost jobs reduce consumer spending, which leads to a further downturn of the economy and more lost jobs.

At least the citizens who still have a job can now purchase products at a cheaper price. Or can they? With no competition, the new retailer has no need to maintain low prices. In fact, why would it? If it buys at the cheapest price it can find and then sells at the highest price the market will allow, there is much more profit to be made for the investors, which entitles top management to pay themselves outrageously high salaries.

A close look at the corporations funded by the stock market will reveal a great many businesses that are more devastating than beneficial. The investors as well can be more devastating to the stock market than beneficial. The monetary value of corporations is increased daily by investment but not because of their investment worthiness. In fact, if investment worthiness were the driving factor, many corporations would be losing value daily. No, corporations are being invested in daily because people contribute to their individual retirement accounts and pay premiums on their insurance. The money has to be invested somewhere!

In the case of 401s and IRAs the money has to be invested somewhere that is acceptable to the Internal Revenue Service, or the investors will not get their tax deductions. The sad thing for the investors is that the tax deduction in many cases is less than their cost of servicing the 401s and IRAs. The real sad thing for the ones at the bottom of the retirement account pyramid is they will never recoup the funds they have invested. The main thing keeping the market value of the corporation's inflated is the need to invest retirement funds. Once people realize how hollow the available investments really are, they will stop contributing and start withdrawing. The stocks will fall to their true value, which is somewhat lower than it was in the sixties before our manufacturing firms started moving off shore.

The first investors to get their money out of the stock market will reap the benefits of the retirement investment phenomenon. These people in all likelihood will be the rich, who have made the base for their fortune by controlling other people's money. The retirement investor will be slow to take action because there are severe penalties for removing funds from their retirement accounts. Funds removed before the age of fifty-nine and a half carry an immediate penalty of 10 percent of the withdrawn funds. An added penalty is realized when the withdrawn funds are added to the person's annual income. The rate at which federal and state income taxes are charged increases significantly as income increases, and the working class investor is unlikely to have sufficient deductions to offset the abnormally increased income.

The reduced price of each corporation's stock will not be of the greatest concern to the corporation represented by the stock. After all, the corporation traded its stock for the money needed to acquire the assets it uses to begin its operation. The big concern for each corporation will be the stock it holds in other corporations because that stock represents the majority of the corporation's cash assets.

Manufacturing corporation stocks will fall along with the tumbling stock prices of every other category of stock. Once the panic is over and the dust begins to settle, manufacturing stocks will rise to the neighborhood of their book value. Although the book value of the manufacturing corporations will be greatly reduced by the loss of their invested capital, it will still be higher than the price the stock will tumble to in the panic, so the price will rise. The holders of the other categories of stock will not be so lucky.

The invested money lost to the manufacturing corporation represents invested profits more so than needed operating capital. Granted the loss of capital may slow its operations, but the bulk of its assets are tangible—they are located in its infrastructure. At the fall, finished products will already be available for sale, raw materials will be in stock, and operating expenses as well as the cost of new raw materials can all be paid for by continued operation.

The medical insurance corporations have contracted with just about everyone in the United States to cover a portion of their medical expenses. After the bulk of the insurance corporations' monetary value evaporates with the tumbling stock market, they will be left with a great deal less money to pay toward the care of the sick and injured. In order to stay in business, they will have to increase their rates during the time of the worst financial hardship the country has ever seen. Most people will not be able to pay the existing insurance rates much less the increased rates. Lack of payment will provide some relief to the insurance corporations because nonpayment breaks the contract of medical coverage. Nonpayment also means reduced income at a time when increased income is greatly needed. The insurance corporations will reach a point where bankruptcy is their only option, and eventually the medical insurance industry will become a sad memory.

The retail corporations that have become very dependent on procuring their wares from overseas require a massive outlay of cash for each shipment of merchandise. The evaporated financial resources from the tumbling stock market will leave them with insufficient funds to invest in new product. They will be able to continue in operation for a time with the stock in their stores and warehouses, but the return from the merchandise on hand will need to cover operating expenses as the on-hand merchandise is being sold. Money for restocking will be too slow in coming and insufficient to maintain full store shelves. The gradual decline of the corporate stores that depend on foreign products will open an opportunity for small non-corporate stores that sell the products of new small local manufacturers to make a comeback, provided they can find the funds and resources to begin operations.

Investments in the stock market can be a great supplement to retirement income. However, as many of the investors in Enron discovered, total reliance on the stock market could end your retirement and force you back to work; provided you are still able to work, and a job you are qualified for can be found.

Before there were 401s and IRAs, many working people set aside a small portion of each paycheck to make investments in the stock market. At the age of retirement, they got a pension from the employer as well as Social Security. The additional income provided by their stocks gave them an exceptional retirement.

Using the derived benefits as an example, 401s and IRAs were developed; presumably so everyone could participate in the boon. The federal government offered tax deductions on the invested money as an incentive to participate.

Employers saw an opportunity to do away with their pension systems by offering to match some or all of the funds deposited into 401s; of course, they protected themselves by withholding full to partial ownership of the matching funds until the worker had been employed for a certain number of years. Each consecutive year of employment, the worker receives ownership of a slightly larger portion of the contributed funds until full ownership is reached, a term called fully vested.

The 401s and IRAs have opened the door to businesses whose purpose is the management of the contributed retirement funds. The investment companies can support themselves and pay massive salaries to their employees by taking a small portion of each customer's investments. But why pay yourself thousands of dollars a day when you can pay yourself millions. By the time a worker is fully vested in his or her retirement system, he or she is paying more each year for the management of the retirement account than he or she is saving on the income taxes through the offered tax deduction.

The massive investment into the stock market generated each month since the inception of IRAs and 401s has caused a continual rise in the market price of stocks. The overall effect is stocks that sell for prices much higher than their true value. The phenomenon is so successful that the stock market continues to rise while the true value of the stocks is falling.

Eventually stock prices will fall to the true value of the stocks. The first signs of this occurring will be the sell-off by the professional investors of all their stock. The entire process will happen quickly; it may take as long as two to three days but probably will happen in less than one day. At the end, the slowest millionaires to respond will become hundredaires, and the people with tax-deferred retirement accounts who can neither access their money quickly nor without penalty will be left with at best a small fraction of the money they were counting on for retirement.

Working people with tax-deferred investments in the stock market such as 401s and IRAs have few options that will allow them to avoid the fall. One option is to withdraw their money early. This will cost them big because they will have to pay income tax on the money withdrawn as well as penalties for early withdrawal. If they are still working, the income tax will be charged at a higher rate because their working income will be added to the withdrawal from their retirement to figure their income-tax bracket.

The taxes and penalties, however, will not be the full extent of their losses. Once the stock market deflates, the country's citizens will have less income for the government to tax. There will also be fewer taxable financial transactions. The government will have less income from taxes, and because of the situation with the stock market, no possibility for borrowing. In order to continue operating, the government will be forced to print money, which will cause runaway inflation. The dollar will lose more and more value as new money is printed.

Another option for those with tax-deferred retirement accounts is to move their money into a gold stock such as IAU or one of the other stocks whose sole holding is gold or silver. Transferring money within an IRA or 401 incurs no penalty or tax liability. As stocks lose value, the smart investors will buy gold and silver. The price of each will skyrocket. During inflationary times, as the value of currency drops, the value of gold and silver remains constant, meaning the price rises in proportion to the inflation.

The ideas in this book can stop the otherwise inevitable inflation. That's not to say we won't see a rise in prices. In truth we may see a massive increase in prices, but they will be accompanied by a corresponding increase in personal income, and eventually there will be a balancing point where everyone can afford to live comfortably—not just a select few. The ideas presented may also stave off the fall of the stock market, but nothing can prevent it entirely because the actual value of most of our stocks is far below the price at which they are being traded.

One sure result from the toppling stock market will be the loss, by millions of people, of their ability to retire. The solution is to make Social Security a true and full retirement system. The chapter on Social Security explains how the system should work as well as how it should be funded.

CHAPTER 17

THE BIG BUSINESS OF FOOD

The massively powerful arm of the US government known as the Department of Agriculture can easily dictate policy to the small farmers of America. The food and chemical corporations that control most of America's farmland, however, are another matter altogether; they use their massive wealth to control the very arm of government that is supposed to be controlling them.

The small family-owned farms that used to produce brussel sprouts, broccoli, green beans, squash, and other health-sustaining crops are rapidly being forced out of business and off their land by corporate farms that produce a single non-nutritious inedible crop. The corporations have the money to apply political clout to enact laws. One such law makes it legal to patent genetically engineered seeds and hybrid plants. Up to this point, patents had not been allowed on plants because as anyone who has battled weeds for control of their yard knows, seeds migrate. Once patented, the agricultural corporations put their seeds on the market and into their fields. The small farmers who purchased the newly developed seeds were forced each subsequent year to buy new seeds from the patent holder. The new patent law included riders that made it illegal for the farmers to use a portion of their yield as seed for the next year's crop, as they had always done in the past. Keeping watch on small farms that didn't purchase their seed, the corporate farmers waited for their hybrids and genetically engineered seeds to migrate into the fields of the small farmers. Once the new plants appeared, the small farmers were dragged into court, where they were kept until their financial resources were drained, and they were forced into bankruptcy, at which time the corporate farms swallowed up their land. The process continues to this day, and if left unchecked the corporate farms will own all agricultural land.

Corporate farms use their political clout to give themselves government-paid subsides that are not available to the small farmers. The subsidies supposedly reduce the price of farm products to the consumer. The money for the subsidies, however, is taken from every worker's paycheck when they pay their taxes. So where's the savings? The true result of the subsidies is that the small farms, which don't produce enough yield to qualify for the subsidies, must charge a higher price for their goods, which puts them at a disadvantage when competing with the corporate farms. In most cases, the smaller farms are unable to sell their yield, so they go broke and lose their land.

The corporate farms use their wealth to run advertising campaigns telling the world's population about the benefits of genetically engineered plants. The advertisements declare increased yield per acre, more health benefits from the improved crops, fewer starving people in the world, and more.

There's a great deal of concern in the world about the potential ill effects to the health of consumers from the new genetically engineered products. In the United States we feel safe because we have the FDA to test our food before it is allowed to enter our markets. Our sense of security in this matter is false because there is very little, and in many cases no, testing required before these engineered foods enter our markets. At the end of this chapter is a chart identifying many of the top agricultural people in our government, including the FDA, who have occupied top positions in the agricultural corporations and vice versa. One would think there would be laws against this obvious conflict of interest, but great financial pressure is exerted on our elected officials, who must constantly seek sufficient funds to retain their office.

Not only do these foods enter our food markets without testing, there is no labeling system to inform the consumer of what they have eaten. So when the number of autistic children all of a sudden explodes, or we see dramatic increases in the number of children with allergies and other autoimmune diseases, no connection is suggested to what the children eat or what their parents, before they were parents, ate. I'm not saying the new food is the culprit, I'm saying no one knows. The very agency on which we depend to make the connection doesn't seem to care. It's entirely possible that new drugs are responsible for the increase in autisms. If you chose to do your own investigating to see how many of our top FDA and Department of Agriculture people have held positions in the corporate food industry, you might as well look to see if the ones who weren't employed in the food industry were instead employed in the drug industry.

In defense of the FDA, I will point out that in an effort to balance the federal budget the number of FDA inspectors was cut drastically in the nineties. The head people in the FDA took the cuts in stride and allowed the drug companies to do their own testing on their experimental products. The food companies were allowed to simply dispense with any test on their experimental products. At least the research and development dollars spent by the drug and food industry are not at risk, even if the health of our nation's citizens is.

Between Nebraska and Illinois there lies a vast field of corn, which covers the entire state of Iowa. A casual observer would think the corn is being grown as food, but they would be wrong because the corn is not fit for human consumption. Livestock eats some of the corn, but you can't really say it is fit for them to eat either. The feedlot cattle, which subsist mainly on a diet of this genetically engineered corn, would die from its consumption within six months if they weren't slaughtered after four months. The bulk of the corn is processed into corn oil and high fructose corn syrup, neither of which has any nutritional value. Granted the consumption of these two products will make you fat, but I repeat there is no nutritional value. In fact, both have decided health consequences from their consumption. The only reason for growing the corn is to make money. A great deal of money is made off the meat of the dying cattle and the products into which the corn syrup is placed. The amazing thing is that no money at all is made off the corn crops. The farmers would actually lose money if they weren't paid off with government subsidies. Yes, tax dollars are forced out of taxpayers' pockets and used to pay farmers to grow crops that not only have no nutritional value but actually create sever health issues for those who consume the crop or anything made from it.

The food corporations have set up shop in many of the third world nations that according to the food corporation's advertising suffer from inadequate food supplies. The corporations force small farmers off their land in much the same way American farmers have been forced off their land. The genetically engineered seeds are planted on land where a variety of wholesome food crops once grew. The population is left with crops that are devoid of nutrition, so the population now truly is starving.

The displaced farmer no longer has the ability to feed his family. His income is gone. His ability to grow food is gone. The poor neighbors that used to trade with the farmer for food no longer enjoy the fruits of his labor. The neighbors, of course, are also displaced, and the fruits of their labor are no longer available to local inhabitants of the villages.

The third world nations into which these food corporations have expanded have higher rates of hunger and malnutrition than they had before. Their children are suffering from the same health issues the genetically engineered food is officially not causing here. Poor country folk who used to get by on the fruits of their labor are now living on the streets of the cities and begging for handouts. The rich of these third world countries have less varieties of food to grace their table, but some have more money in their pocket to make up for the loss of their large variety of safe, healthy, edible food.

Genetically engineered crops and new agricultural laws are not the only way the citizens of the United States are being abused by the food industry's meddling with our government. The food industry has sent its representatives to Washington to offer its services, which relieves some of the cost of such things as figuring out the recommended daily allowances for our different food groups. It even helps the government by creating the food pyramid, which is used to show what a well-balanced diet looks like.

A whole section of the food pyramid is dedicated to dairy products because as we all learned in school that milk is high in calcium, and calcium is needed to build strong bones and teeth. We all know this as a fact because we were taught this in school. The reason this information is available to us in school is that our government allows the dairy association to advertise in the schools. In fact, they have so much influence in our government that it is a requirement that milk be provided with all school meals. Why complain about such legislation? It makes sense, after all, because milk is so good for us. Or is it?

Studies have shown that the consumption of animal protein is required in order for many forms of cancer to grow in the human body. One of these studies used the protein from milk alone to show that the cancer growth could be controlled simply by increasing or decreasing the quantity of milk protein ingested. The levels used in the test were within the normal range of human consumption, and when the milk protein was eliminated from the diet, replaced by plant protein, the tumors ceased to grow and began to shrink. The milk industry totally neglects this research in its advertising.

Likewise the dairy association says nothing about the fact that the consumption of dairy products causes plaque to grow in human arteries and leads to heart disease. It bases all its advertising on the well-known fact that dairy products help build strong bones and teeth, which, by the way, is false. Tests have shown that dairy products create an acidic condition in the human body. To correct this condition, the body uses all of the calcium provided by the dairy products that caused the acidic condition to partially neutralize the acid. The robbing of calcium from teeth and bones fuels the rest of the neutralization process. So consumption of dairy products actually weakens bones and teeth.

Other scientific research has shown a link between the consumption of milk and the development of type 1 diabetes, as well as multiple sclerosis. Obviously not everyone that drinks milk will suffer from these diseases. Genetic research is finding that everyone is predisposed to different diseases based on their genetic makeup. Milk is simply the catalyst that activates these genes, and only upon interaction of certain other events and or genes, some known and others still under study.

The fact is that cow's milk is absolutely the best food in the world for baby cows but when consumed by humans is extremely detrimental to their health. So why are dairy products afforded an entire section on the food pyramid? Our government allows the food industry to control the recommendations for our daily food consumption.

The Cattlemen's Association also sends it representatives to Washington to sit on the panels that determine our recommended daily allowance of the different food groups. Its section of the food pyramid includes protein from all the animals, including fish, as well as beans. The beans, of course, actually are good for human consumption and do not promote heart disease or provide the needed ingredients for the growth of many forms of cancer. The same cannot be said for anything else in the food group, yet we are led to believe that a certain percentage of our daily diet should come from animal protein if we are to be healthy.

The FDA is supposed to be protecting us, yet food is the leading cause of death in America. The deaths that occur immediately following consumption are the result of the failings of FDA inspectors or rather the lack of Inspectors. However, the majority of deaths caused by food take a shortened lifetime to occur. The food-induced deaths are slow and painful in coming. The growth of the fast food industry is directly and indirectly responsible for many of these long-term food-induced deaths yet the FDA has done nothing to alert the public to the dangers, much less mitigate the dangers the nutrition-deficient foods pose. The meat factories, a direct result of the fast food industry, are a blatant failing of the FDA. The first of these to appear should have been shut down immediately by the FDA. Instead we are warned that E. coli is a natural danger of meat, so the meat must be cooked long enough and at sufficient temperature to kill the E. coli. In fact, E. coli is not natural at all. It comes to us as a result of the feedlots, another failing of the FDA. Corn is not a natural food for cattle. In fact, it slowly kills them through the formation of E. coli in their stomachs. The antibiotics, which are serving to breed antibiotic-resistant harmful organisms, prolong the life of the cattle imprisoned in the feedlots but doesn't kill the E. coli. The FDA does nothing while these E. coli breeding cattle stand around in their own excrement and the excrement of other infected cattle for months while the cattle fatten. (The excess fat is one of the killers of Americans, but it increases profit to the cattle industry.) The sick dying cattle reach the meat factory with their excrement-covered coats and are introduced into the factory by having their rear legs connected to a conveyor system that pulls them off the ground and delivers them to slaughter and then on into the factory with their filthy coats intact. The removal of their coats while the process of cutting begins delivers E. coli into our meat supply. The dissecting and removal of the entrails delivers more E. coli contamination. An FDA whose true purpose was to protect American citizens wouldn't have allowed any of this process to come into existence, much less allow it to continue.

Salmonella is introduced into our food supply by contaminated eggs and chickens. Egg-producing chickens are caged for their entire lives in small cages where their waste droppings cover their food as well as the eggs they lay. The eggs roll across the slopped feces-covered wire mesh, providing the bottom of the cage, and onto a feces-covered conveyer that takes the eggs to the collection point. The FDA warns us not to eat raw eggs rather than making sure the salmonella doesn't end up in the eggs in the first place. The chickens that are raised for their meat live wing to wing in temperature-controlled barns for their entire lives. Of course, freeing the chickens so that they can live a normal life that precludes the formation of salmonella would cut into profits, which are needed for campaign contributions and lobbying.

Dual Loyalties Table

William D. Ruckelshaus - Chief Administrator U.S. Environmental Protection Agency
William D. Ruckelshaus – Board of Directors Monsanto Corporation

Michael Taylor – Staff Attorney FDA 1976-1981
Michael Taylor – Lawyer King & Spaulding 1981-1991 (client Monsanto)
Michael Taylor – Legal Advisor / Deputy Commissioner for Policy U.S. FDA 1991-1994
Michael Taylor – USDA Administrator of the Food Safety & Inspection Service 1994-96
Michael Taylor – VP for Public Policy Monsanto Corporation 1996-2000
Michael Taylor – Senior Advisor of FDA Commissioner 2009 - 2010
Michael Taylor – FDA Deputy Commissioner for Foods 2010 -

Lidia Watrud – Ecology Division U.S. Environmental Protection Agency
Lidia Watrud – Biotech Researcher Monsanto Corporation

Terry Medley – Administrator Animal & Plant Health Insp. U.S. Dept. of Agriculture
Terry Medley – Director of Regulatory & External Affairs Dupont Corporation

Margaret Miller – FDA Deputy Director of Human Food Safety (1989 – Present)
Margaret Miller – Monsanto Corporation Chemical Lab Supervisor (1985 – 1989)

Michael Phillips – Agriculture Board Member National Academy of Science
Michael Phillips – Head of Regulatory Affairs Biotech Industry Organization

Jack Watson – Chief of Staff to the President – Jimmy Carter
Jack Watson – Attorney Monsanto Corporation

Clayton K. Yeutter – Secretary U.S. Dept. of Agriculture
Clayton K. Yeutter – Board Member Mycogen Corporation

Larry Zeph – Biologist Office of Prevention U.S. Environmental Protection Agency
Larry Zeph – Regulatory Science Manager Pioneer Hi-Bred International

David W. Beier –Chief Domestic Policy Advisor to Al Gore
David W. Beier – Head of Government Affairs Genentech Inc.

Linda J. Fisher – Assistant Administrator EPA Office of Pollution Prevention 2001-2003
Linda J. Fisher – VP of Government & Public Affairs Monsanto Corporation 1995-2000

Michael A. Friedman M.D. – Commissioner U.S. Food and Drug Administration
Michael A. Friedman M.D. – Senior Vice President for Clinical Affairs G D Searle & Co.

L. Val Giddings – Biotech Regulator U.S. Department of Agriculture
L. Val Giddings – Vice President of Food and Agriculture Biotech Industry Organization

Marcia Hale – Assistant to the President Director for International Affairs
Marcia Hale – Director of International Government Affairs Monsanto Corporation

Mickey Kantor – Secretary U.S. Department of Commerce
Mickey Kantor – Member Board of Directors Monsanto Corporation 2000 - 2002

Josh King – Director of Production White House Events
Josh King – Director of Global Communications Monsanto Corporation

Clarence Thomas – Attorney Monsanto Company 1976 – 1979
Clarence Thomas – Supreme Court Justice 1991 – Present

Donald Rumsfeld – US Congressman 1962 - 1969
Donald Rumsfeld – CEO G D Searle & Co. 1977 – 1985
Donald Rumsfeld – Secretary of Defense 2001-2006

John Ashcroft – Missouri Senator 1995 -2001(received record donation from Monsanto)

Robert Shapiro – CEO Monsanto 1995 - 2000
Robert Shapiro – President Clintons Advisory Board

Wendal Murphy – North Carolina State Senator 1989 – 1993
Wendal Murphy – Smithfield Board Of Directors (2000 – Present)

CHAPTER 18

CORN

The elimination of America's ability to feed itself began in the laboratory of a chemical company. This laboratory developed a herbicide to kill plants and at the same time developed a plant that would not be killed by the herbicide. To ensure the company's ability to recoup its investment in the research and development, it sent some of its top executives to Washington, where they found new employment. The company also hired lobbyists to influence the legislators that were not prior employees of the company.

Laws were made that allowed the patenting of seed, a practice that was heretofore not allowed, for one reason because plants migrate on their own. The argument was made that the developer of such a valuable plant deserved to recoup the research and development investment. The well-placed former company people together with the influenced legislators ignored the fact that the new plant was inedible and had almost no nutritional value. They also didn't take into consideration that seeds migrate, and farmers, in order to stay in business, use a portion of their crop to produce seed for next year's crop.

The newly patented seed and herbicide was advertised to farmers. The advantages advertised by the chemical companies induced many farmers to buy seed for the first time in years. The next year, when the farmer attempted to save seeds for replanting, they found out for the first time about the new laws allowing seed patents. Legal action was threatened, and the farmers were forced to purchase seed for their next year's crop. Those farmers that refused to purchase the patented seeds and chose instead to purchase unpatented seed from farmers that had not purchased the newly patented seeds were unmolested for their choice. It was not until the new crop came up that representatives of the patented seed company showed up to point out the fact that volunteers from the previous year's crop were growing alongside the unpatented plants.

Litigation was not just threatened but carried out. The farmer who was already having financial trouble from the purchase of seed for two years in a row was now forced to pay a lawyer to represent him in court. The result of the litigation in most cases was financial ruin for the farmer before the case was finished in court. The farm or a portion of it was sold to pay for the overwhelming bills. The purchaser of the forfeit land in almost every case was the chemical company that developed the herbicide and seed.

The new patent laws were not the only thing the farmers that purchased the patented seed and herbicide found out about when their first crop was harvested. Tasting the fruit of their new genetically altered plants revealed a harsh taste and tough texture. The farmer immediately realized the tables of America would no longer welcome the fruit of his yield.

Animal feed was the only outlet for the genetically engineered produce. The animal feed market was flooded with corn, and the price fell. Many farmers were forced to sell off land to pay their bills, and the chemical company that started it all was there with its checkbook at the ready to purchase the land.

All was not lost; a new market was formed. The new corn, although inedible, was well suited for the production of high fructose corn syrup. Although the corn off the cob had a bad taste, the high fructose corn syrup made from the corn could be used to improve the taste of other products. As the high fructose corn syrup production grew, more and more products were found and created in which it could be used and soon high fructose corn syrup replaced cane and beet sugar in many soda pops and numerous other sweets.

As more farms used the new herbicide and compatible seed combination, the fortune of the chemical company continued to grow. Some of the money was used to fund teams that spent their time driving around in search of fields to which the genetically engineered seeds had migrated. Some fields infected with the migrating seeds were much easier to spot than others. A corn stock growing in a field of brussel sprouts, for instance, can be seen with no more than a glance.

Teams of lawyers were hired with a portion of the newly acquired profits. The lawyers spent their time suing the farmers whose field had been invaded by the migrating genetically engineered seeds. It didn't matter that a farmer, growing broccoli, had no desire to have corn invade his field. The fact that it was there gave the chemical company grounds to sue for lost compensation. In most cases, the farmer was kept in court long enough to be financially destroyed.

A very large portion of the chemical companies' profits were used to purchase the land of the financially besieged farmers. The newly acquired land was sprayed with the new herbicide to kill everything that once grew there and planted with the genetically engineered herbicide-specific resistant seeds. As the amount of land dedicated to growing inedible corn grows, the land available for growing edible nutritious crops decreases. As a result, more and more of the produce found in the corporate-owned grocery stores is imported from other countries.

The corporate growers of genetically engineered corn can boast a higher yield per acre than the edible high-starch hybrid of yesteryear. That doesn't make the genetically engineered herbicide-resistant corn any more edible. It has, to be kind, a less than favorable taste and absolutely no nutritional value. In fact, the edible variety of the hybrid corn that has been around for more than seventy years that we all think of as a nutritious vegetable is actually one of the less nutritious vegetables.

The millions of acres of farmland that are used to grow the new genetically engineered corn are wasted. It cannot even be argued that the land use turns a great profit, because the corn is actually grown at a financial loss to the growers. The chemical companies that now control most of our farmland have sent their lobbyists to Washington to ensure legislation that provides subsidies to the farmers that grow the inedible non-nutritious crops the chemical company has patented. In other words, government subsidies, paid for with tax dollars forced from the pockets of the working class give the corporate farms financial support to cover their losses and provide a profit.

The subsidies allow the corn to be sold at such a low price that the factories that extract the high fructose corn syrup can pass the saving along to the manufacturers who use the high fructose corn syrup in their products. This allows the producers of fattening non-wholesome food to sell their products to the consumer at a lower price than the consumer pays for fresh wholesome produce.

The vast stretches of land that now grow the genetically engineered corn at one time grew the variety of vegetables our population needs in their daily diet to have and to maintain healthy bodies. Growing a variety of healthful produce, of course, would not be practical for the corporate farms that use massive machinery and very little manpower to prepare the land, plant their crops, and distribute their chemical herbicides, pesticides, and fertilizers.

The genetically engineered seed, the chemical fertilizers that provide a limited supply of the nutrients needed by the plants, the chemical herbicides used to rid the planted fields of weeds, and the chemical pesticides that kill the bugs the nutrient-poor plants cannot fight off on their own are not cheap, but since they are all manufactured and distributed by subsidiaries of the same conglomerate that owns the corporate farms, the money per se is all kept in the family.

In order to grow the variety of crops the people of our country need to have healthy bodies takes a great deal of manpower. The soil must be prepared in a particular way for each vegetable grown, and each crop must be planted differently. At harvest time the process varies for the reaping of each fresh ripe vegetable. The type of farming to grow the country's needed variety of vegetables cannot be done with the mass production technique used to grow genetically engineered high-yield inedible corn.

The fact that the corn is inedible in no way prevents it from finding its way into our food supply. High fructose corn syrup, one of the main substances derived from the inedible corn, is found in almost every processed food gracing our grocery store shelves. The process that changes a portion of the corn into high fructose corn syrup does not magically make something edible from something inedible. The high fructose corn syrup is just as inedible as the corn from which it is derived. It does, however, taste much better, once diluted in processed food. That is the reason it is used so extensively.

The high fructose corn syrup, because of its subsidies, is a cheap replacement for cane and beet sugar. This makes it more desirable to manufacturers of processed food. Sugar, of course, has been known for years to cause ill effects once introduced into the human body. Causing the body to get fat is the most obvious of these but not the most devastating. An extensive list of health issues is associated with the consumption of sugar.

The chemical makeup of high fructose corn syrup is exactly the same as sugar, $C_6\text{-}H_{12}\text{-}O_6$. The damage done to the human body by the consumption of either substance is exactly the same. The high fructose corn syrup, however, has one additional effect. It blocks the receptors that tell the brain that the stomach is full. This means the consumer, in the mistaken belief he or she has not had enough to eat, consumes more food and thereby increases the profits of those who sell the processed food.

The genetically engineered inedible corn indirectly makes its way into our food supply in other ways as well. It is processed into feed for livestock. The byproduct of the corn fed to cattle is even less edible for them than the corn or its derivatives are for humans. A cow will die from the consumption of corn. The process takes about six months. However, the consumption of the corn byproduct makes the cattle fat in a relatively short period of time, which results in higher profits. So the cattle are fed corn byproducts for about four months and then slaughtered. The fattened cow is far less healthy for human consumption, but the profits are higher, and that is all that matters to our corporate meat producers.

Not all the genetically engineered corn makes its way into our food supply. A portion of what remains of the corn after the processing is distilled into alcohol to become a fuel additive that increases the quantity of fuel while reducing its price per gallon. Note this savings is not passed on to the consumer; it is merely a way of increasing profits. Alcohol is water-soluble. Conversely, water can be held in solution in alcohol even when that alcohol is mixed with a petroleum product. Water will not dissolve in petroleum-based fuel without alcohol added. The fuel will float on the water. If water, whether liquid or vapor, finds its way into the fuel tank of a vehicle with purely petroleum-based fuel and then the water makes its way into the engine of the vehicle, the results will be immediately apparent in the operation of the engine. The engine will at the very least run rough but may possibly quit altogether. With the addition of alcohol to the fuel, the water will dissolve in the alcohol and run through the engine without notice. In the short term this is a good thing. However, in the long term the engine will rust out from the inside. This is bad for the owner of the vehicle but very good for the car manufacturer. Note the alcohol added to fuel actively induces water vapor from the air into the fuel. It is no longer a chance induction that can and usually is prevented.

There are no benefits to the general population in the growing of genetically engineered corn. There are simply detriments. To the rich corporations of the world, however, there are a great many benefits, all of a monetary nature. That is why the genetically engineered corn is grown in great quantities on the land that was once used to grow a variety of health-sustaining long-term life-giving vegetables.

CHAPTER 19

CONSUMABLE INEDIBLES

Consumable inedibles is seldom if ever uttered, while fast food is a common term. Fast food, however, is a misnomer because food provides nourishment. There is no nutritional value in the products sold for consumption at fast-food restaurants. Food is supposed to help our bodies rebuild worn out cells. Food is supposed to contain enzymes to help our bodies digest the food. Fast-food establishments process out all of the nutrients and enzymes from their products before offering them for sale. Fast food does have the necessary ingredients to fill our fat cells and, in fact, contributes greatly to the fattening of America, but that hardly qualifies it as food. Consumable inedibles is a much more descriptive term for the products sold at the establishments where millions of people regularly stop for a quick bite. But, of course, a term such as "consumable-inedible restaurants" would hardly be effective in drawing money from the pockets of customers, and, in truth, fast-food restaurants are in business for no other reason than to extract money from the pockets of hungry people.

Another place to find consumable inedibles is at your local grocery store. They are the products that have been processed to the point that all of the nutrients have been removed or destroyed. Slow-acting poisons are added to these products in order to give them a longer shelf life. These products are filling to your stomach and your fat cells. They do not, however, enable your body to heal itself, grow new cells, or replace its worn-out cells.

The engineering of herbicides that kill all plants except one has been done for many of our commercial crops. The plants grown from these genetically engineered seeds are generally beautiful plants with visually appealing fruit. Most of the fruits of these plants are devoid of taste and nutrition, but the process is not meant to provide a nutritional delicious plant. It is meant to produce money, and that it does very well.

There is no need to weed the fields, which have been saturated with the compatible herbicide before and often during the growing of the plant. The easy maintenance allows fields to be truly massive in size, creating the savings that come with economy of scale. The tons of beautiful whole fruits and vegetables virtually spring off the grocery store shelves ahead of the less visually appealing nutrition-filled organically grown tasty fruits and vegetables.

A main ingredient common to most consumable inedibles is high fructose corn syrup, which in its pure state is much too sweet to enjoy eating. It is added to give taste to the flavorless over processed consumables. Genetically engineered seeds such as wheat, corn, and soy are ground to powder and formed into concoctions that can be processed into a variety of shapes—flat noodles, macaroni noodles, spaghetti, couscous, cereal, bread, chips, donuts, muffins, cakes, stuffing mixes, and much more.

High fructose corn syrup is not only used to flavor the processed food found in grocery stores but is also found in many fast-food products. While it has no nutritional value, it does provide a great many empty calories, but, more importantly, it blocks the receptors that tell our brain that our stomach is full. This is great for the fast-food restaurants because the customer ends up consuming a great deal more product and thereby parts with a great deal more money.

The fast-food industry has gotten so big that massive meat processing centers have been built to keep up with the demand. The new, bigger, automated meat processing centers have now managed to run all of our local meat packing plants, which used to process the beef from local ranches, out of business. The massive meat processing centers get their beef from feedlots where cattle stand around in their own excrement and get fat eating processed genetically engineered corn that is not fit for human consumption. The feed made from this corn is toxic to the cattle. A steady diet of the feed over a period of six months would kill them. The solution is for the meat processing center to bring the cattle into the factory after four months of eating the feed, kill them, and then process them for shipment to the fast-food restaurants or your local supermarket.

The free-roaming cattle raised on the ranches that used to supply the local meat packing plants are now sent to the feedlots as part of their processing. The result is that only those lucky enough to raise their own beef and those that live in a small town where a local butcher shop can still be found are able to get healthy beef with a low fat content to grace their dinner table.

The fast-food industry has taken away our ability to get wholesome beef and has contributed to the fattening of many Americans. It would seem the FDA would get involved and outlaw feedlots as well as put some requirements in place that force the fast-food industry to serve wholesome food. The meat processing industry and fast food industry, however, are both multimillion-dollar businesses, and the FDA has shown time and again it is more concerned with the financial health of large American businesses than it is with the physical health of the American people.

The very least that should be done is to set some standards that require a substance to be both wholesome and nutritional before it can be called a food. The current drive-through eating establishments that sell quickly available consumable products that are neither nutritious nor healthy to eat should assume a new term, such as "consumable inedibles," which is more truthfully descriptive than "fast food."

CHAPTER 20

CATTLE

The cowboy, a favorite character of the Old West, lived on a diet rich in beef. Vegetables were rarely if ever included in the cowboy's diet. These tough, hard-working men died young. The hard work and rough life were blamed for their hearts giving out. The farmers of the day worked just as hard, and quite possibly harder, than did the cowboys, yet the farmers lived longer. The difference in lifestyle, indoor family living, was the factor attributed to the longer life. The farmer's diet, rich in vegetables grown in his own garden, was never considered as a reason for the longer life expectancy.

The cattle of the Old West were raised on the land, where life was tough. They roamed the range looking for food. They were as lean as the cowboys that tended them. In the final months of their lives, they traveled a great distance to reach a railhead. On the drive, any fat they may have gained on the range was worked off. They entered the railway stock car for the trip East lean and hungry.

Cattle today are raised on land thick with edible grass, and feed rings filled with hay overcome any shortages. The cattle are fattened on the land, and in the last months of their lives they are sent to feedlots to gain more fat before they are slaughtered.

The feedlots are small and crowded. The cattle stand around in excrement dropped by themselves and others. Their muscles atrophy from lack of use, which makes their marbled meat tender. Their day revolves around the feed troughs filled with corn-based silage. The digestive system of cattle doesn't handle corn well, and as a result E. coli forms in their digestive tracts. They depart the feedlots with their hide coated with E. coli infected excrement.

Upon arrival at the meat factory, their hind legs are connected to a conveyer that pulls them off the ground for slaughter and processing. Their life organs are pulled from their body cavity, and their feces-filled coat is cut from their meat as they move inverted toward the butchers. E. coli, spilled from damaged digestive organs and rubbed from the tarnished hide, coats the meat as it is cut into pieces. Anything from the process that doesn't classify as a marketable piece of meat on its own is cast into a vat for grinding into hamburger. While an individual piece of meat may escape contamination, there is no hope for the leavings that process through the grinders.

Today E. coli is an accepted part of meat departing the processing factory. Warnings to eat only well-cooked meat are the norm and are well-known. No longer can meat be purchased at a grocery store, brought home, unwrapped, placed in a frying pan, immediately flipped, just as quickly removed from the frying pan, placed on a plate, and safely eaten. The very thought raises alarm bells in every modern person's head. However, as recently as the 1960s it was common practice among many to eat their meat very close to raw. In fact, some body builders swore that eating raw meat was best.

By the 1960s the FDA was well established and had a strong presence in every facet of the food industry. The many meat-processing establishments were no exception. The presence of FDA inspectors was so common that a casual observer would have thought the person was part of the regular staff. The inspector barked, and the managers made sure the inspector's orders were immediately carried out because the bite of an inspector meant the doors were closed until the changes he required were made.

Over time, food industry lobbyists have made suggestions to elected officials that a reduction of FDA inspectors would be a good way to save taxpayer dollars. A massive reduction of FDA inspectors was seen under the Clinton administration as a measure to balance the federal budget. A continued reduction since that time has left the ranks of FDA inspectors so weak that an inspector is rarely seen in most food factories. Further lobbying has been successful in limiting the power of FDA inspectors. The combination is one reason the presence of E. coli has been able to creep unchecked into our meat supply.

In a business where the main focus is making small pieces of meat out of big ones, there is a great deal of potential hazards to the workers. Workers sustained many horrifying injuries before they were able to establish unions and bring about safety rules and legislation. The formation of OSHA in the 1970 added assistance to the unions in keeping the workers safe.

The fast-food industry has placed such a high demand on the meat industry that meat processing has been industrialized. A small number of these massive meat factories have replaced the numerous meat-processing centers. Safety concerns reduce profits for the meat factories. Lobbyists have been successful in keeping OSHA fines small and potential prison sentences even smaller. Hiring undocumented workers that can't organize or complain about their working conditions for fear of deportation has defeated the unions.

Lean is a relative term. The FDA recommends the consumption of lean meat daily. No part of the cattle that are intentionally fattened to maximize profits can be truly termed lean. There are, however, portions of the cattle that have the fat cut off, and there are vats of cattle parts that have less fat introduced. The hamburger from the vats with less fat and the cuts of meat that have been trimmed of fat are what is in the packages labeled lean.

Modern medicine is credited with a longer life expectancy. Considering the American public's high consumption of fat-laced meat, there is simply no other explanation. Blood pressure medicine, high cholesterol medicine, bypass surgery, and even heart transplants are all absolutely necessary to keep the people alive that fill their veins with the flesh of fat cows. Skinnier cows and strong warning against their mass consumption would be a better measure for public health, but these measures would reduce profits for the cattle industry and medical industry alike.

Pills and exercise are the preventative measures for heart disease, and surgery is the cure. Diet is mentioned by some, but it's not really pushed as a preventative measure, much less an absolute cure by those responsible to the American people, such as the FDA and the American Heart Association.

Studies have proven that the consumption of beef contributes to heart disease, yet the FDA recommends that it should be consumed daily. The misinformation is so ingrained that almost any American will tell you that beef must be consumed to ensure the body gets its required protein. They might even point to the lean, tough, short-lived cowboys of yester year as proof that a diet high in beef is healthy.

The FDA lists milk and the products derived from milk as healthy foods that should be consumed daily. The dairy association stresses that growing children must drink milk because the calcium contained in milk is necessary to build strong bones. They also recommend that adults drink milk to maintain strong bones. Research has shown that milk creates an acidic condition in the human body. The body uses calcium to neutralize this acidic condition. The process consumes all of the calcium from the milk and then takes the remainder of the calcium needed to finish neutralizing the acid from the bones. The fact that the consumption of milk actually causes bones to deteriorate doesn't seem to deter the dairy association from making its false claims, nor does it cause the FDA to speak out on behalf of the American people.

Deteriorating bones is not the only detrimental effect milk has on the human body. Studies have shown that the consumption of milk by products causes a buildup in the blood stream of plaque that leads to heart disease. These studies are not hidden from the American people, but neither are they advertised.

On the other hand, the misinformation about the benefits to the human body from the consumption of beef, milk, and the byproducts of milk are highly publicized. The reason for publicizing this misinformation should be obvious; a great deal of money is made annually off of all of these products. The mystery is why the government agencies supported by our tax dollars don't tell us the truth.

The answer is simple. The businesses that make millions of dollars annually from the sale of these products pay lobbyists to inform our elected officials about all the good information they have gained from their biased inaccurate research. The agencies that have spent millions of dollars provided by grants and universities to do the research that proves the truth of the health detriments have no money for lobbying. In fact, to use funds that were appropriated for research to lobby our elected officials with the results of the research would be a misuse of the appropriated funds.

As long as we allow big business to control our government through campaign contributions and lobbyists, we will continue to be given misinformation. Furthermore, laws will continue to be written to the benefit of big business and to the detriment of the majority of the population.

In more recent times, the health detriments of milk and beef have been increased. In an effort to increase the yield without increasing the milk cow population, cows are filled with antibiotics and milk-producing hormones. The effects of the hormones are passed on to those who consume the milk. Girls develop breasts at a younger age, and their breasts grow to a much larger size in the same way as the milk sacks of modern dairy cows. The antibiotics injected into beef cattle and milk cows alike are contributing to the formation of antibiotic-resistant germs.

Research, concluded more than twenty years ago proved the need for the consumption of animal protein and for that animal protein to be present in the human body before many forms of cancer can grow. The research is outlined in "The China Study," a book written by the lead researcher, T. Colin Campbell, PhD, and his son, Dr. Thomas M. Campbell, MD. Every effort made by Dr. Campbell and his team has been blocked from reaching official status of fact in the agencies within our government that should be advising us of this most relevant data, and, of course, as stated, there is no money available to lobby for something that could be so costly to industry.

CHAPTER 21

THE BIG BUSINESS OF MEDICINE

The townspeople once paid their doctor set compensation for his services. His house, which included adequate space for his work, as well as his supplies and equipment, were provided. Anyone requiring medical treatment was cared for, free of charge. Medical care, free of charge, is as it should be. After all no one gets sick or injured just so he or she can enjoy the services of a medical professional.

As cities grew and times changed, the doctors started charging for their services and paying for their own housing, work space, and equipment. Getting sick or injured created an additional bill at a time when it was least convenient. The advent of medical insurance meant that a relatively small monthly payment could eliminate a somewhat larger expenditure at an unpredictable and decidedly inconvenient, stressful time. The insured or one of his family members that suffered the pain of injury or sickness didn't have to worry about the cost of treatment rendered because the insurance company would pick up the tab.

The new insurance was available at a reasonable price to anyone who cared to purchase it. The idea caught on and became very popular. The doctors running their small practices as well as the doctors in charge of hospitals saw an opportunity to increase their personal income by increasing the cost of their services. The insurance companies didn't mind.

The increased cost of medical treatment was good advertising and enticed more people to purchase the new insurance.

The increased patronage of the medical insurance companies offset the rising cost of medical care for a while, but eventually the insurance companies decided they needed to increase their rates to maintain what they felt was a fair profit. The increased cost of medical insurance caused some customers to reconsider, but the ever-increasing cost of medical treatment left them with little choice. Medical treatment was no longer something a working-class person could afford without help.

The doctors were the first to see the availability of higher pay for their services, but their realization was just the beginning of the trend toward higher profits for those involved in medical care. The doctors in charge of the hospitals saw an opportunity to increase the charge for everything the hospital provided. The providers of everything the hospitals used from bedpans to high-tech equipment wanted in on the hospitals' increased profits, so they increased their prices. The hospitals had no choice but to pay the increased prices. They responded by increasing their prices to maintain their newfound profits.

The insurance companies had to cover the increasing prices, but they didn't want to give up their profits. They increased their rates enough to cover their cost plus a little more to increase their own profits. The nurses saw everyone around them getting more money in their pockets and unionized to demand their share. Workers of other trades saw an opportunity to use their unions to their advantage as well.

The trade unions negotiated with the insurance companies to come up with group rates for their members. An increase in union dues, which amounted to far less than the workers were paying out of their pockets for medical insurance, freed the workers from paying for medical insurance. The unions, of course, did not take the entire cost of the insurance on their shoulders. The unions, as is their nature, forced employers to pitch in on the cost of medical insurance. Soon it was the trend that all employers, whether their workers were unionized or not, paid for their employees' medical insurance.

The doctors in private practice started to see increased cost for all of their supplies and equipment. To maintain their newfound profits, they had to increase their rates to cover their increased costs, but, of course, the increased rates had to include a little extra profit for their troubles.

Hospitals, in addition to being a place to care for the sick and injured, became big business. Hospital administrators, whose background and education were in business rather than medicine, took over leadership from the doctors. Everything was streamlined and accounted for to ensure the greatest profit. Any business school professor will tell you, "The purpose of a business is to make a profit." Care of the sick and injured became secondary to the importance of profit. The medical industry was born.

The medical insurance industry increased its rates, but it didn't stop there. Hospitals were sold liability insurance, and doctors were sold malpractice insurance. The increase in operating cost from the payment of insurance premiums was passed on to the patients with, as is usually the case, a little something added for increased profits. The increases in the cost of medical treatment led to an increase in medical insurance rates.

Employers decided to share the cost of medical insurance with their employees. A portion of the monthly insurance rate was deducted from the employee's paycheck. The insurance companies decided to share the cost of medical care with patients. A percentage of the cost of the medical treatment, known as the deductible, was passed on to the patient.

Eventually the insurance companies came up with copays, a flat fee paid by the patient before any treatment is given. The copay might pay a very small portion of the treatment or the entire cost of the visit. A visit for an injection that cost $30 with a 20 percent deductible and a $25 copay actually results in the medical facility receiving an extra $1 profit, and the insurance company that has been receiving $800 a month to insure the patient incurs no cost at all.

Today the combined lifetime fees, monthly payments, copays, and deductibles are higher than the entire adjusted-for-inflation cost of a lifetime of medical treatments prior to the advent of medical insurance. The worker has gained nothing from the advent of medical insurance and lost much.

Medical insurance has managed to eliminate the word *care* from the medical profession. We can no longer call it medical care because those who administer the insurance companies and medical facilities really don't care. It has become medical assistance to those that can afford the combined cost of insurance payments, copays, and deductibles. Medical insurance has facilitated the evolution of medical care into the medical industry, but what has the medical insurance business evolved into?

The medical insurance leadership is housed in multimillion dollar high-rise buildings where they administer the vast fortune they have accumulated. The executives are paid multimillion-dollar salaries; they travel in private jets, and they relax in extravagant company-owned estates. The medical insurance premiums paid to the medical insurance corporations do not pay for medical treatment. The medical insurance premiums are invested, and medical treatment is paid for with a small portion of the returns from those investments.

The perpetrators of medical insurance bask in a life of luxury while their customers as well as those who cannot afford their disservice are left with a medical system that extorts money from the sick and injured. Those that can afford medical insurance as well as the copays and deductibles are not guaranteed the medical attention they require. The medical insurance industry, even though its employees have no medical training, reserves the right to determine what treatment a patient may receive.

Drug therapy generates billions of dollars in pharmaceutical income. Modern medical schools are controlled by the pharmaceutical industry and are greatly influenced by the consumable inedibles industries, which is why drug therapy is taught and nutrition is not. How can we trust doctors that spend hundreds of thousands of dollars on their education and learn little or nothing about nutrition?

Nutrition is the single most important factor in determining a person's health. People who eat right *do not* suffer from chronic illness. They don't develop diabetes, they don't suffer from heart disease, they don't have high cholesterol, they don't get fat, they don't get some forms of cancer, and they are of absolutely no use to the medical industry.

Poor nutrition, a massive asset to the medical industry, generates millions of dollars to each of the various producers of consumable inedibles. Various food producers donate the DVDs and literature, which accounts for the bulk of, and in some medical schools the entire curriculum that is dedicated to nutrition. Some, but not all, medical schools offer classes in nutrition, but taking the offered classes is not a requirement for graduation.

Millions of people annually participate in fund-raisers to research various diseases. Their intent is to eradicate the dreaded disease. Thirteen percent of the collected money must be spent on the research for which it was collected. The rest of the money can be used for the administrative costs of collecting the money such as setting up the fund-raiser, distributing the funds to various research labs, and massive paychecks for the administrators of the fund.

Modern medicine is all about making money and is ill-served by a healthy public, so most of the money that actually goes into the commercial research laboratories is used to develop treatments, formulate drugs that can control the disease, develop chemicals that can kill diseased cells, and run tests on the developed products and procedures. The medical research revolves around treatment rather than prevention or cure because treatment develops an income stream and prevention and cure do not. Once the drugs and chemicals are tested and released for sale to the medical industry the price to purchase them includes a little something extra to recoup the research and development cost, which includes the portion received through donation. In essence the medical research industry is laundering the donated money in order to turn it into income.

Thousands of health studies have been conducted and many more will be done in the future. There are so many, in fact, that it's hard to know which are true and which are not. They cannot all be true because the results of some disprove the results of others. Unfortunately for those of us that seek the truth, all it takes to initiate a study is money.

Any moneymaking entity can use its resources to fund a study that proves its product is good, healthy, safe, nutritious, or effective. The research can be manipulated to show whatever findings the funding agency wants to prove. Experiments that would disprove or invalidate the findings can be left out of the research process. Who is to say how the money is to be spent if not the financier?

A third party that wants to dispute the finding must pay for their own research to prove their point, and when they do, who is to say which research we should believe? The consumers, even if they have the knowledge to understand the research, rarely have the resources to check it. They are left to accept the conclusion presented or be confused by conflicting conclusions. One university study that shows eating meat is bad for you is countered by three meat industry financed studies, which show that eating meat is good for you.

Sometimes claims are made with no research done. Calcium is a main ingredient in cow's milk, and the bones and teeth of the human body consist mostly of calcium, so drinking cow's milk must be good for humans. Right? The theory has been accepted probably from the moment it was first proposed. The dairy association, with its obviously good news, has been allowed by our government to advertise its product in our schools. Students in public school have been taught from a young age that drinking milk is good for them. The students grow up, have children of their own, and tell their children, "Drink your milk; it's good for you."

Researchers financed by government grants, studying autoimmune diseases, have found that the consumption of cow's milk is a necessary ingredient in the process of developing type 1 diabetes and multiple sclerosis. Other research has shown that the consumption of cow's milk actually robs human bones and teeth of their calcium. It would be a misappropriation of funds to use grant money provided for research to advertise the findings of the research. Therefore, the new research is available but not widely publicized. The supposed health benefits of milk, however, are widely publicized by the dairy industry because there is a great deal of money to be made from the continued sale of cow's milk.

We the people expect the FDA to watch out for us, and we expect the news agencies to let us know about every new discovery. So if they don't tell us there's a problem, there is no problem. Our trust is so complete that we don't even consider the fact that the watchdogs of old may have been infiltrated by those we expect them to report on or are simply influenced by money. In actual point of fact, both are true.

The news agencies that we trust so completely to inform us of any wrongdoings or new developments that could have significant impact on our lives are in business to make money. The focus of their business may be to pass on information, but the main purpose and the reason they are in business is to make money. A news story that could have significant impact on an industry's ability to make money is quickly dealt with at the corporate levels. The effected industry leaders commune with the news agency leaders and come to an understanding of what stories should not be made public or how to squash a story that may have slipped out without prior consideration. The unfortunate release of a story may be remedied by updates to the story that change the findings to the benefit of those with money on the line, and then the story disappears and is never heard about again.

We all know that there are lobbyists in Washington and that no one is elected without first spending vast quantities of money on their campaign, yet somehow we believe that our elected officials and the leaders they appoint to run the various government agencies always keep the best interest of the majority at heart when passing legislation or running their agencies. We seem to be assured that our elected officials are uninfluenced by those that contribute to their campaign and remain loyal to us.

Nothing could be further from the truth. The top officials at the FDA are not only influenced by lobbyist of the pharmaceutical industry and the food industry, but many of the top officials actually used to work for one of these two industries, and other top officials expect employment in one of the two industries when they leave government office.

Wheat, soy, and corn are now the top commercially grown crops in America. The seed of all three have been genetically engineered to provide more profitable crops. The chemical companies that engineered the seeds have engineered companion weed killers that are lethal to every other plant. The engineered seeds grow into a plant that when eaten by insects, which have short life spans, will cause a lethal autism in the third generation of the insect's offspring, thus reducing the time the crop is exposed to the insects.

The plants have also been engineered to produce the highest yield possible. The plants as well as the ground they grow on are chemically treated with spray herbicides, pesticides, and fertilizers. The FDA has determined that since these crops are essentially the same crops that were growing before the engineered seed or special sprays were developed, there is no need to test any of it to determine if it is safe for human consumption. The significant rise in autisms, type II diabetes, and other diseases since the sale of the yield from these engineered crops has no proven connection but then no one is checking to see if there is a connection.

The FDA has adopted the same laissez-faire attitude toward new pharmaceuticals. They have allowed the manufactures of new drugs to do their own research and provide the findings to the FDA for approval of the new drugs. The fact that 106,000 Americans die each year from drugs that are properly prescribed and administered seems to be of no concern to the decision makers at the FDA.

Millions of dollars are donated every year to find a cure for cancer. Americans who volunteer their time and money to these fund-raisers are hopeful that a cure will soon be found. The research, however, is not geared toward a cure but rather treatment of cancer because treatment equates to profits, and there is no money to be made by the medical industry from healthy people.

Heart disease is another illness to which millions of dollars are donated each year for research. Again, the money goes toward researching treatment rather than searching for a cure. The cure, of course, is irrelevant because the prevention of heart disease is well known and advertised. The first step is to severely limit or eliminate the consumption of animal protein, and the second step is to eliminate all the processed food made from corn, soy, and wheat from our diet.

To figure out if modern medicine places more importance on helping the sick and injured or on making money, one need only look at the statistics. Approximately 39,000 people die each year from unnecessary surgery. Obviously not everyone who receives an unnecessary surgery dies as a result. In fact, the percentage of people that die each year as a result of unnecessary surgery is relatively low, about one-half of 1 percent. There are an estimated 7.5 million unnecessary surgeries performed each year. The major benefactor, and in most cases the only benefactor, of these surgeries is the surgeons that make exorbitant amounts of money to perform the surgeries and the owners of the medical facility in which the surgeries are performed.

Approximately 106,000 people die each year from adverse drug reactions brought on by drugs that were prescribed and properly used.

Approximately eighty thousand people die each year in hospitals due to infection.

From 80 to 90 percent of patients admitted to the hospital are admitted for issues caused by or related to bad nutrition. Nutrition is the single most important factor contributing to the state of a person's health, yet 26 percent of patients leave the hospital more malnourished than when they arrived. Less than 6 percent of graduating physicians in the United States receive any formal training in nutrition, which means they are never taught things like consuming 3,000 milligrams of niacin a day, which can be found in two handfuls of cashews, may control depression. They are taught instead to prescribe drugs (even though some of the side effects of certain depression drugs can be horrific) because drugs produce the greater profit.

The medical profession has evolved from free care to being prohibitively expensive.

In the process, the caring has been reduced and in some case disappeared altogether, replaced by greed. The first question, when you walk into a medical facility is, "How are you going to pay?" That is followed at length by, "What is your chief complaint?" Blood spurting from an artery may reverse these questions, but don't bet your life on it.

CHAPTER 22

OUR WALL STREET GOVERNMENT

Our place in the world is slipping away while our leaders place their emphasis on helping their rich campaign contributors get richer. Our elected officials and their rich friends are all so busy spending their ill-gotten fortunes they don't even see us settling into our third world position below the up and coming industrial giants on this planet. The voters overwhelmingly believe they need do nothing because our elected officials have our best interest at heart and, being much smarter than the average Joe, are better able to lead our sinking country back to prosperity. Those voters that are awake and realize how close we are to losing our position in the world feel powerless to do anything about it.

"Government of the People," a noble idea of recent history, has never materialized as a viable entity; in fact, the world is and always has been controlled by the wealthy individuals that make up a small percentage of the population. A news reporter a while back made the statement on national television that the working class has no representation in Washington, DC, because they have no lobbyists. How true this statement is, and how sad it is that it's taken for granted that our federal government caters to those with money rather than the masses who vote.

As this book is being written, our supposed representatives in Washington are carrying us toward a fiscal cliff. The Republican representatives of the people want to maintain tax breaks for the wealthiest 2 percent of our citizens, while the Democratic representatives of the people want to maintain tax breaks for the working class, who make up the majority of the population. The debate is fueled by a need to have sufficient funds to operate the government while leaving enough funds in the economy for it to continue operating.

Taxes are only part of the possible solutions being discussed. There are many spending cuts on the table. Each of the proposed cuts will negatively affect a very large number of voters. The elimination of subsidies to private industry and other pork barrel spending that would affect only a few voters is not even up for discussion.

In a true democracy there would be no issue. The 2 percent that control the majority of the money would not only lose their tax breaks but have their taxes raised because they most certainly do not represent the majority of the citizens; in fact, as stated, they only amount to 2 percent of the populations. Furthermore, any cuts in federal spending would be directed toward negatively affecting the fewest voters possible.

The very rich use their influence over politicians to have laws made that favor the wealthy. Tax laws are biased toward the rich and are so complex that a tax lawyer is needed to decipher them. Our elected officials would have us believe the tax breaks for the rich are designed to encourage the rich to create jobs. It seems to have entirely escaped everyone's notice that through the 1970s and into the 1980s most US manufacturing jobs were exported to countries with cheaper manpower. No amount of tax breaks will bring these jobs back. The tax breaks for the rich accomplish nothing more than hastening the arrival of the day the United States defaults on its loans.

It should be painfully obvious to those of us that make up the majority of the population of the United States that the small minority that controls the majority of the money in the United States, and thereby our government, cares nothing for the country or its citizens. Their only interest is in increasing their wealth and, in effect, their power.

Banks are supposed to be a safe place where we can store our money. The Great Depression led to a great deal of controls placed on banks to prevent the reoccurrence of their failings. However, deregulation of the banks brought about through lobbying and campaign contributions has eliminated the controls and opened the door for bankers to return to their old tricks, one of which is to use depositor money to make risky investments. Riskier investments return a higher yield on the investment. The banks offer a set interest rate on money deposited in savings accounts. The return on investments over and above the interest paid to the depositor belongs to the bank. The natural tendency is for the bankers in the upper echelons to use the excess income to pay themselves massive salaries and give massive bonuses to the bank employees who handle the transactions that bring in the highest returns.

The massive salaries and bonuses account for only a small percentage of the return on investment. The extra income received from return on investments leaves the bank with more money to invest. The pursuit of larger returns leads to riskier investments. Sometimes the risk pays off, and sometimes it doesn't. A bad investment means the employee handling the investment doesn't get his bonus, but the upper echelons still get their massive salaries as long as the overall trend is success in the risky investments.

This may look like gambling, and if that is the conclusion you have reached, then you are absolutely correct. Very few gamblers win all the time, and banks gambling with their depositors' funds are no different. A series of risky investments losing money all at once can leave a bank with insufficient funds to continue operating. The bank at this point must close its doors and go out of business. The depositors lose their savings, and the bank employees from the tellers to the upper echelons must look for a new job, but, of course, the upper echelon bank employees and the employees that handle investments get to walk away with the millions of dollars they were paid for making the risky investments. The big losers are the depositors, who had no idea what was going on with their money.

In 2014 the new laws that are supposed to improve the American medical industry will go into effect. At that time, it will become mandatory that every American citizen have health-care insurance. There is no law that says they have to have food to eat, warm clothes to wear, or shelter from the elements. They must pay for health care above all their life-maintaining needs because the rich medical insurance corporations have influenced our elected officials to enact laws that put more money into the insurance company coffers. The insurance company, of course, will still have the right to refuse payment for life-saving medical procedures.

Working-class citizens vote for our elected officials, and their vote is decisive, but they have little or nothing to do with picking the candidates who are going to run for office. People and entities with lots of money make that choice with their campaign contributions. The rich entities that decide who is going to run for office send their lobbyists to Washington to inform "our" elected officials of the entity's wishes. The worst part is that not all of these entities and rich individuals are Americans.

Corporations exercise a great deal of control over our government, much to the detriment of private citizens. Corporations push laws into existence that help them make more profits and pay less tax. In a government of the people, each citizen is afforded one vote, no matter their income. A corporation is made up of individual citizens, all of whom have a vote. To allow the corporation to influence our government is in effect giving the individuals who run that corporation extra votes. Indeed, they are actually taking control from the voters by deciding who will be the candidates and in effect the lawmakers of our country. They further control our government by paying lobbyists to influence the lawmakers.

The plant Patent Act of 1930 made it possible to patent new varieties of plants in the United States. The wealthy US agricultural corporations lobbied to make it possible to patent hybrid plants. Up to this point, patents had not been allowed on plants because as anyone who has planted a garden knows, seeds migrate. The conglomerate soon put their patented seed on the market and into their fields. The farmers who purchased the newly developed seeds were forced each year to buy new seeds. The new patent law made it illegal for the farmers to use a portion of their yield as seed for the next year's crop as they had always done in the past.

The drug companies have used their considerable wealth to pass laws that force the FDA to allow the drug companies to do their own testing of their drugs. Every year hundreds of thousands of Americans die from prescription drugs that are legally prescribed and properly taken. Doctors, heavily influenced by the drug companies, regularly push drugs on patients whose major problem is they have a poor diet. Their vitamin and mineral poor nutrient-starved bodies, rather than getting the sustenance their ravaged bodies crave, are given drugs that will create new problems for which more drugs can be prescribed, except, of course, in the cases where the side effects cause the patient's death.

Ask almost anyone, and they will tell you, "The United States has a democratic government." By definition, a democracy is a government in which the people exercise the supreme power directly or indirectly through a system of representation usually involving periodically held free elections.

Unfortunately, elections are not free. They cost millions of dollars per candidate. Granted the term "free election," used in the definition means the voter is free to elect the candidate of his or her choosing, but the fact that a massive quantity of funds are required in order to be a candidate often precludes having a candidate the majority of the population would choose, so in effect they do not have a free election.

It's impossible to have representation of the majority of the people when the only candidates that can afford to run are the candidates who are representative of the minority of the population. Therefore, the United States does not have a true democracy. It has a mock democracy or, if you will, a government of the money.

The candidates, in rare cases, use only their own money to run their campaign. Most candidates, due to the extreme cost, do not have sufficient funds to run their campaign, so they are forced to use a portion of their own money in conjunction with other people's money to run their campaign. While a good deal of campaign money comes out of the pockets of individuals, the majority of the money needed to run a successful political campaign comes from corporations.

Corporate dollars used for advertising are the controlling influence over who becomes a candidate for public office and who does not. This fact gives corporations, which are inanimate individual entities, more control over our electoral process than the people, who are individual human voters. The candidates, once elected, must do the bidding of the corporations that influence their campaigns or risk the inevitability that there will be a great deal of negative advertising to overcome during their next election. Term limits could help this situation, but to really give control of our government to the people, we must take money out of politics.

Consider the detriment of corporate control over our government.

The national debt can be directly attributed to corporate influence. Many corporations make enough profit every year to fall into a 50 percent tax bracket. However, the tax laws are such that most massive corporations pay little or no taxes. It's ironic that even the money they pay to fund campaigns, which gives them the power to demand the tax breaks, is tax deductible. Ineffective taxation of major corporations is not the only contribution large corporations are making to our national debt. A major portion of our government expenditures goes directly into the pockets of corporations.

Defense contracts are a good example of where much of this money goes. The generals at the Pentagon decide what our military needs, only to be overruled by elected officials who have no concept or concern about national security. These elected officials, following the wishes of their campaign contributors, direct purchases to be made based on the desires of the campaign contributors. These same contributors demand American tax dollars be given to foreign governments, who in turn purchase military equipment to be used for the control of their starving population.

Government subsidies are another way massive corporations drain money from the government coffers. The airlines, some of the nation's biggest corporations, charge extravagant prices plus a great deal of extra charges for their services, yet our elected officials find it necessary to also give them a portion of our tax dollars in the form of subsidies. The railroads are paid subsidies from our government's coffers to do nothing. In turn, the railroads ignore the potentials for their expansion, which could bring them high profits while reducing the country's need of foreign oil. The government pays a great deal of money to corporate food suppliers, which is supposed to make food more affordable to those with reduced income.

It doesn't seem to occur to anyone that these subsidies are paid with tax dollars collected from the same people that are buying the food. The worst of these subsides, which are paid in the name of reducing the cost of food, are paid to the corporate growers of corn that has been genetically engineered to the point that it is no longer edible and is in fact used for other purposes.

The reduced taxes, the government contracts, and the subsidies all contribute to the national debt, but, really, what is the national debt, who demanded it, and why is it still growing? The national debt is the sum total of all the bonds the government has sold in order to continue operating when collected taxes are not enough. The bonds are bought by anyone with money to invest. Individuals buy government bonds as part of their retirement account, and in return the government pays interest to help that individual retirement account grow. However, corporations, including the corporate banks, make the largest purchase of government bonds. Why would corporations pay taxes to fund the operation of the government, when they can loan money to the government to fund its operation and then collect interest while maintaining ownership of their money?

Corporations use their influence over our elected officials to encourage government spending. A great deal of the government's money is paid to the corporations, but no matter where the money is spent, the spending creates the need for the government to sell bonds, which the corporations quickly snatch up and use to increase their income.

A growing national debt is just one of the many detriments the people of the United States have suffered by letting corporations take control of our country. Corporate manufacturers have eliminated smaller privately owned manufacturers. This hurts not only the business owners who lost their companies but the customers as well because the large corporations don't care enough to produce quality products. In a corporate world, where you are farther removed from your customer, profits are of far more importance than customer satisfaction, especially when the corporation has taken a considerable share, and in many cases all, of the market away from its competitors.

As the corporations grew, the unions of their workers grew, and they started demanding more money. In the name of fair trade, the corporations used their political influence to eliminate tariffs on foreign goods. No one seemed to be the wiser as the corporations abandoned their domestic factories and built new factories in third world countries where labor was still cheap.

The inferior quality of manufactured goods is something the younger generation of Americans takes for granted if they notice the problem at all, but unemployment is something we all notice, and we have the corporations to thank. Isn't it ironic that our elected officials tell us they must reduce corporate taxes in order to create jobs? How can the corporations create jobs when they shipped their manufacturing processes overseas? Of course, if the elected officials want to keep their jobs, they have to satisfy both sides, so they create laws that give tax breaks to the corporations and tell the voters the tax breaks will create job.

As we all know, not all of the manufacturing corporations moved their operations overseas. The automobile manufacturing corporations, for example, still have most of their factories here in the United States. They still pay the high wages and, of course, low taxes. What they don't do is listen to the American people, who are sick of paying high prices for fuel to operate their automobiles. We ask for electric cars, and the best thing the car companies can offer is a hybrid, a vehicle that only gets about 30 percent better gas mileage than a vehicle with a conventional gas engine. One would think the oil tycoons are the major stockholders of the automobile corporations. The electric cars the car companies finally started building have a limited range with no means for recharging the batteries while driving. The vehicles are small, overpriced, and useless for extended trips.

I heard a news report a few years back about a guy who converted his Detroit built V-8 engine to get 80 miles per gallon. Then I never heard another word about it. I might count the story off as a hoax, if I didn't personally know of a Boeing engineer that designed a carburetor that could get 80 miles per gallon from a V-8 engine. He sold his idea to one of the big car corporations, and none of us have ever seen the results of his invention. I suspect the guy I heard about on the news sold his idea as well. After all, just because a guy is smart enough to build a better car doesn't mean he can afford to build it, much less mass produce it. Look what happened to Tucker. He had the means, and the established automobile corporations still shut him down.

As long as we allow corporations to select the candidates who will become our elected officials, we will be at the mercy of the corporations. Modern technology could build a full-size car that has sufficient battery power to drive two hundred miles and incorporates a hydrogen-driven constant speed generator that can fully recharge the batteries in half an hour. The car companies, however, will not build a vehicle like this because if they did the oil companies will see an end to their massive profits. Furthermore, through their massive almost tax free profits as well as their political influence, they will make sure nobody else puts a practical electric car into mass production.

There seems to be no limit to the damage done by people hiding behind corporate law. One of the ways corporate entities gain financial power is through bankruptcy. It is quite common for a corporation to build itself with debt. As the corporation grows, so does the debt. Once the debt begins to take too much of the profits, the corporate leaders form a new corporation and begin transferring assets to the new corporation. The original corporation is then forced into bankruptcy, leaving the suppliers as well as the stockholders with nothing but a shell. This process should meet all the criteria for fraud, but through corporate influence of our laws, loopholes have been made to avoid prosecution.

It may seem that I am totally against corporations, but this in fact is not the case. What I am against is letting corporations rule our government.

Bribery of an elected official is illegal, as is coercion to force an elected official to do one's bidding. However, campaign contributions are legal and necessary to finance today's massively expensive campaigns. It would be almost funny if it weren't so detrimental to our democracy that simply changing the name of a thing can make it legal.

Candidates for office often try to make it clear they are committed to fulfilling the will of the voters. They spout slogans and make promises about all the good they will do once elected. It's human nature to be thankful to someone who helps you. If that someone gives you millions of dollars to help you achieve your goal, then it should be no surprise to anyone when you return a favor with any means within your power. The voters show outrage when campaign promises are not kept, and the government continues with business as usual, but that's the end of it; come the next election they vote for the incumbent.

Lobbyists are paid by special-interest groups to influence our elected officials. The lobbyist and the elected official sit down together over a meal that costs hundreds of dollars, which is paid for by a benefactor of both. During the discussion, the desires of the benefactor are made clear along with the promise to give or withhold campaign funds depending on the outcome of the elected official's efforts toward making the benefactor's wishes come to pass. The process, which is nothing less than coercion, is considered legal. The meal over which they discussed business is even tax deductible

Anyone who studies law quickly comes to a conclusion that is not readily apparent to the average person. *Laws are not fair; they are just legal.* The people who accept campaign contributions and sit down to expensive meals paid for by others make laws that are unfair to the majority and legally advantageous to the minority.

As evidenced by regular announcements and ongoing legislation, our elected officials are very concerned about the American medical industry. A great deal of our tax dollars are regularly spent to ensure medical insurance is provided to those who cannot afford it on their own. It seems to me that an elected official who was not being influenced would build a hospital where a poor person could get medical care for free rather than give tax dollars to an insurance company. After all, when was the last time you ran to your insurance agent for help when you were sick or injured? Our elected officials tried to create legislation to make the health insurance companies stop the practice of refusing coverage and dropping clients who are sick. The end result was a new law that says everyone must have medical insurance. Keep the campaign contributions flowing!

Millions of American taxpayer dollars are donated to countries where a large portion of the population is disadvantaged and starving.

A disadvantaged, starving population will soon die without help. It has nothing to lose and will, with its dying breath, often attempt to overthrow the government that does nothing to help it. Some of the donated American taxpayer dollars are paid to food corporations to feed the starving population. However, a great deal of our tax dollars are paid to corporations that provide arms to the foreign government's army in order to keep the starving people under control.

Often we are led to believe that our elected officials have our best interest or the best interest of others in mind while they bend to the will of those who pay for their campaigns.

Why is it that the American government spends billions of dollars helping foreign governments with their problems while millions of Americans suffer? Government jobs are being lost daily due to lack of funds. Joblessness nationwide is at epidemic levels. The number of homeless people has for many years been shameful for such a rich nation, and now their numbers are growing. Millions of people have no access to medical or dental care. Having a job is no defense against homelessness or hunger because many jobs don't pay a living wage. Health care is so expensive that even people with above-average incomes can't afford it. Those who have health-care insurance are not guaranteed health care they can afford. The care they need may be refused by their insurance company, and even if approved, the copays and/or deductibles may very likely be more than the insured can afford.

So why are our elected officials sending our hard-earned dollars to foreign countries to help with their problems instead of solving the problems of American citizens? Our elected officials give varied answers to this question. We must help the homeless, hungry, and sick citizens of the poorer, less fortunate nations in this world. We must give aid to maintain world peace. There is no end to the lame reasons (lame because the money sent seldom if ever fixes the problem cited). To find the real reason one need look at where the aid money is spent. The money trail is not easy to follow. In some cases it's impossible to follow, but rest assured it ends in the pockets of those who donate to campaigns and spend a great deal of money lobbying. In some cases, it ends in the pockets of the elected officials.

Government building contracts is one pathway through which elected officials move money out of the pockets of taxpayers and into the pockets of campaign contributors. Government building contracts include profit. The person who bids on and wins a government building contract generally never puts a day's labor into building. They simply take our tax dollars by the millions and then pay out thousands to have other people do the actual work. Our elected officials have argued for years that contracting is cheaper for the taxpayer, but is this really true?

The contractor and the government both need workers to accomplish the task. Does the contractor pay his employees less? I spent thirty-two years working for the government; for many of those years I was involved with planning and construction, both in-house (government designed and/ or built) and contracted. I can tell you that in general the contract workers were much better paid than the government workers.

The contractor and the government both need to buy materials. Does the contractor get his building materials cheaper than the government? They might if they are a large contractor and do most of their building in the same area. However, keep in mind that the government always buys its building materials from the lowest bidder.

The contractor needs to make a profit to stay in business. Does the government pay itself a profit? They better not, because if they do, someone needs to go to jail.

The other thing required to build a building is the land to set it on. The contractor plays no part in acquiring the land. Therefore, the cost of land is the same no matter who builds the building.

Using these simple comparisons, it's hard to figure out how anyone could figure it's cheaper for the government to pay a contractor to build a building than it would be for the government to use its own labor and resources.

The cost of employee benefits is one of the places where the government accountants work their magic. They figure in medical insurance and retirement. The civilian contractor may also pay these expenses, but they are not the worry of the government and are therefore ignored. The specific cost of these benefits that the government attributes to each job is difficult to figure, so it's hard to argue that the amount they assign is unreasonable, but it is.

Another thing the government figures into its cost is tools and equipment. The cost of tools supplied to the government worker is figured into each job, which of course is ridiculous because they use the same tools for every job they do. Most civilian workers supply their own hand tools, and even though the company supplies the heavy equipment, it is of no consequence to the government, so, again, these items are ignored when figuring the private business costs and weighed heavily in the government cost.

A final point: the government accountants do all their calculating to compare the cost between in house work and contracting using the bid price of the contract. However, the final cost of almost every government building contract includes cost overruns. These overruns in some cases could double the cost of the contract because once the contract is awarded to the lowest bidder, there is no need by the contractor that wins the bid to keep the price of his change orders low.

CHAPTER 23

EMPEROR MONEY

Money has left its station of servitude and taken over as emperor. Every candidate for public office knows the more funds available for campaigning the more likely the candidate will have success at the polls. Incumbents of public office understand they must carry out the wishes of those who contribute campaign dollars or suffer the consequences of insufficient funds for reelection. As long as we let money control elections, we can only pay lip service to democracy. If we the people ever want to have a true democracy, we need to take money out of politics. Suggestions for how this process might work are offered in the chapter entitled "Free Elections."

The emperor's influence is decisive in the election process, but his influence goes far beyond politics. Decisions are regularly made based first on the availability of money. Available resources; the right, correct, or just course of action; even the will of the person making the decision are all secondary considerations to how much money is available. Money was invented as a tool to make it easier to exchange goods and services within an economy. Placing more importance on it than that leads to all sorts of incorrect decisions. One need only look around to see this is true.

An artist splashes paint thinner in his eyes, loses his eyesight, and is instantly potentially unemployed. The same day, two blocks away, a man is involved in a car crash and is rushed to the nearest hospital, where he later dies. The eyes of the dead man, who was an organ donor, are undamaged and are a perfect match for the newly blinded artist. Both men are in the same hospital. All the resources are available to remove the dead man's eyes and give them to the man in need. Does the hospital immediately take action to restore the blind man's sight? No, there are financial considerations that must be addressed.

Every day there are people who die with perfectly good organs. In all but a very few cases, the organs are placed in the ground or burned. There are literally thousands of people whose lives could be made better by receiving these wasted organs, but money, or rather the lack of it, prevents the transplants from taking place.

The medical field is full of similar situations where the availability of a patient's money takes precedence over what should and could be done for the sick and injured. The travesty doesn't stop there. Many horrible life-changing diseases could be prevented, but emphasis in the medical community is placed on treatment rather than prevention because treatment creates the largest money stream.

The emperor demands a fair, or rather unfair, piece of itself for each gallon of gasoline purchased by automobile drivers. The nasty little secret goes much deeper than the obvious fixing of gas prices through the commodities market. Vehicle engines are purposefully designed to use the maximum quantity of gasoline that public opinion will allow. Numerous inventions over the past fifty years make it possible to get close to 100 miles per gallon of gasoline from a V-8 engine. The rights to each invention are either purchased outright by the gasoline industry or are subdued from production in some other way. In the last twenty years technology has become available to build vehicles that use no gasoline. These vehicles could run on electricity and recharge their batteries while in transit with small constant speed hydrogen-driven engines. Presently not a single one of these vehicles is in production because the emperor long ago saw the wisdom of using oil money to gain power over the car-producing companies of the world.

Space travel is another area where money considerations are dominant in the decision process. However, if you stop to think about it, the actual physical resources needed for space travel are extremely limited compared to resources available. The real cost in our efforts to travel in space is greed.

Every company that sells anything connected with space travel places the highest price possible on their commodity because they know the price will be paid from the deep pockets of NASA.

NASA's pockets, although deep, are not bottomless. They are, in fact, only filled with as much money as can be appropriated from the federal budget. In tough economic times, less money is budgeted. So at this point in time the decision on whether we travel in space, to what degree, and how far we go is based solely on money available. The fact that we must get off this planet in order for us to survive indefinitely as a species is not even considered.

Whether we should survive indefinitely as a species is a valid consideration for discussion. Whether it is up to us to decide whether we survive as a species is another valid topic for discussion. You might even find it interesting to discuss whether there are uninhabited habitable planets for us to inhabit. Discussion about whether there is enough money available for us to pursue our indefinite survival as a species, however, is ridiculous. Not because there is an unlimited amount of money available, but rather the resources needed, save one, are in adequate supply. So what we really need to discuss is how to alter our economic system so that available resources can be used where there is a valid need to use them.

That one resource, by the way, that is needed but in short supply is nuclear energy; at this point in time it is the only power source we know of that can take us the distance we need to travel in order to actually make a difference to ourselves in the pursuit of our longevity as a species.

Granted the day the Earth is destroyed by fire from our sun going nova is still a few million years away, but it may take every bit of the time we have left for us to establish ourselves on distant planets, and to get there we need nuclear energy. Of course, if we use nuclear energy to destroy the Earth, a fate that could take place any day, then we end the consideration of our longevity immediately. We may also end our potential indefinite longevity by unnecessarily using up our nuclear energy as a hazardous terrestrial power source.

As stated, materials needed to build spacecraft are available and in adequate supply; in fact, as we reach out into space more physical resources will become available. Knowledge at this time is still growing, and much more needs to be acquired as we make improvements in building spacecraft. It can be argued that the pursuit of knowledge requires money, but knowledge is an inexhaustible resource, so letting it be limited by money is absurd. I don't mean to distract you with my thoughts about space travel. I'm simply using it as one example to show how preposterous it is to let money maintain its position as emperor.

There are more down-to-earth, direct, and immediate considerations that affect our everyday lives, and one of these is our police forces that serve and protect our towns, cities, counties, states, and country. All of these police departments are facing cuts to their personnel and equipment. Not because our country is becoming a safer place to live but because there are insufficient funds to pay the highly trained officers. Emperor money determined long ago that certain crimes against the general population were not important enough to prevent by the apprehension and incarceration of the criminals that perpetrate these crimes. Crime scene investigation techniques are constantly being improved, but they are not employed for residential break-ins where only theft is involved. The emperor has also limited response to potential residential break-ins where the only sign of a break-in is an automatic alarm. Long ago he eliminated the foot patrols that make it difficult for a thief to wait in a dark alley for an unsuspecting citizen to walk by.

Daily we hear news reports about further cuts in our police forces. These cuts are brought about by further reductions in the funds available to the administrators of our police departments. Even though the prevention of murder has long ago lost its importance to the emperor, until recently the investigation of murder has maintained one of the highest priorities. Now, however, even that has changed. A recent news broadcast announced the elimination of the section of the department that investigates "cold cases." It seems the emperor has now determined that a murder that has gone unsolved for a length of time is no longer important.

Elected officials, who regularly make the determination to direct public funds away from police departments try to help in the prevention of murder by passing legislation that limits our Second Amendment rights.

They seem to be of the opinion that laws against possessing and carrying guns will influence the criminals that ignore the laws against murder. They are probably right about these laws having an influence on criminals. The criminals, who once had to fear that innocent citizens might be carrying a firearm, would become emboldened by the assurance that their intended victim is, by law, unarmed.

The job of "serving and protecting" the public is made more difficult by the emperor's insistence that the mentally ill pay for their care or go without. The cost of mental care for a child in need could easily financially devastate a household. So loving parents do what they can for their slightly to severely disabled child until that child reaches the age of majority. At the age of majority, the child has the right to go out on his or her own without regard for the wishes of the parents. Consequently, there are adults among the general population who are mentally incapable of providing for themselves; many of these individuals have mental issues that prevent them from understanding the difference between right and wrong.

Citizens who are mentally incapable of getting and holding a job are nevertheless responsible for acquiring the food needed to keep themselves alive. Furthermore, they must find shelter and provide themselves with clothing. The emperor demands that all of these items be paid for by the individual receiving them or by someone else in his or her stead.

The mentally ill are oftentimes forced to steal so they may stay alive. Sometimes they simply beg to receive food and clothing. Shelter they find under bridges and in doorways.

Some mentally sufficient individuals chose to join the league of the homeless; others are forced by the emperor's declaration that a certain level of unemployment is good. Whatever reason each homeless individual has for living on the streets, the emperor demands he or she be there. This demand is not made in the form of a proclamation but rather by our system of economics that does not ensure that every citizen who wants a job can have a job that pays a living wage.

Jobs that do not pay a living wage regularly force mothers to make the decision of what they feed their children based on what their food budget will allow rather than what is most nutritious for their children. It has been scientifically proven that a diet high in fruits and vegetables is optimal for human development as well as the healthful maintenance of the human body. However, fresh fruits and vegetable are more expensive than less healthy foods such as processed carbohydrates and hamburger.

Cattle that are raised for their whole life in their natural habitat and eat their natural food are much better for human consumption than those that are fed the leftovers of processed corn in the last months of their lives. Likewise free-range chickens that eat a wholesome diet are much better for human consumption than are the chickens raised their whole lives shoulder to shoulder in temperature-controlled buildings where they are fed a variation of the same corn leavings as are the cattle. However, the corporate-owned grocery stores generally offer only the less nutritious meats because they provide the greater profit. Mothers who can find the time in their busy schedules to shop around, may find a better choice of meat at local family-owned butcher shops, but they must pay a price that the meager leavings of their small paycheck might not support.

Most people would agree that fast food is far from healthy. People eat it because it is convenient, fast, and cheap. What most people don't realize, however, is that packaged food that is cheap to buy and easy to make is no more nutritious than the fast food purchased at drive-through restaurants.

In order to have any food at all to feed their children, most mothers find it necessary to work. Pre-school-age children, however, do not take care of themselves. Working mothers, therefore, must find someone to take care of their children while they work. In some cases a family member, such as a retired grandparent, is available to attend to the young children. In most cases, however, working mothers must pay for day care. The day-care cost can easily eat up most of the mother's income.

Children who have reached an age sufficient to attend school are no longer in need of paid day care for the majority of the day. They can sit in their overcrowded classroom and watch their underpaid teacher try to maintain discipline. From time to time the mostly unnoticed children learn something. The besieged emperor ignores the pleas of teachers and parents alike to reduce class sizes and increase available teaching resources.

The emperor, however, recognizes opportunity when it presents itself. He strengthens himself by increasing taxes on the working class with promises of improving education and then does nothing for education with the added revenue, choosing instead to fund government contracts and subsidies, which are prime examples of how the emperor siphons public funds into private pockets.

The main focus of this book is to present a new economic system that takes money out of the driver's seat and places it back in the toolbox where it belongs. Changes do not happen in a vacuum. Every occurrence of change causes other changes. It is, therefore, necessary to look for the whole series of changes in order to ensure the occurrence of positive changes and the prevention of negative changes. Keeping this in mind may help the reader better understand the proposals presented in the second half of this book. At some points the reader may look at individual proposals and say the author is proposing we institute socialism, and at other places the reader will be sure I am proposing we turn communist. To truly understand the concept I am proposing, please consider the contents of this book as a whole. Once this is done, the reader may indeed see pieces of socialism, capitalism, and communism incorporated into the new economic system, but they will also see some concepts that have never before been incorporated into any economic system because these concepts totally eliminate the ability of the few to use money to control the lives of the many.

CHAPTER 24

GUN CONTROL

Good gun control starts with a complete understanding of the operation of your gun. The operator should be capable of completely dismantling the gun, cleaning it, and reassembling it without confusion or assistance. The sights are of particular importance to a handler that is operating a new gun for the first time. Once a person is completely familiar with the operation of the gun, has disassembled it, cleaned it, reassembled it correctly, taken it to a safe location with a good backstop for the discharged projectiles, and ensured his or her hearing and eyes are properly protected, only then should the person fire the new gun for the first time.

The first few shots can be made without concern for hitting the target exactly. Once the handler is comfortable with firing his or her new gun, then he or she can assess whether the sights are set correctly. This is done by carefully aiming at a precise point on the target and then verifying that each progressive projectile hits the exact same point. From there, the user can adjust the sights accordingly until the fired projectile consistently hits the precise point at which it was aimed.

Some guns have fixed sights that cannot be altered. The shooter of a gun with fixed sights follows the same beginning familiarization procedures up to the point of seeing where the projectiles consistently hit, at that point, the shooter practices compensating for the flawed stationary sights. If the projectile hits three inches to the right and two inches above the intended point of impact, then the shooter changes his or her aiming point to three inches to the left and two inches below the intended point of impact. Once the shooter can consistently hit an intended precise point on the target, then he or she can consider the familiarization and practice completed for the day.

Proper gun control demands the shooter return to a safe shooting location regularly, daily if possible, until he or she can consistently hit the target from the first round fired to the last. Thereafter, the shooter should schedule regular practice sessions to maintain good gun control.

Gun control doesn't end with good shooting. Every gun owner should be clear on when to use a gun and when to leave the gun in its holster. The military is very good at teaching all service members proper handling of weapons. Unfortunately, not every citizen has the privilege of serving. The NRA offers very good training courses that every gun handler should attend, whether prior military or not.

Legislating gun control has resulted in rooms filled with unarmed innocent citizens, any of whom might be a gun owner that has left his gun at home because of the legislation, being exposed to a mentally deficient armed person or persons who don't care about the legislation.

When I was a child, before the present gun control laws were in place, the principal of my grammar school carried a .38 caliber pistol in a shoulder holster. There may have been other members of the school staff who carried weapons as well. I don't know for sure because I never saw their weapons. I only saw the principal's gun one day as he was about to give me a well-deserved swat with the paddle he kept in his office. I didn't see the weapon because he showed it to me. I saw it because he moved in such a way that his suit coat opened enough for me to catch a glimpse of it.

Nothing ever came of the principal or any other staff member caring a weapon to my grammar school. The point is the gun or guns were there, and if a crazed gunman had shown up to kill us kids, the principal would not have vainly laid his life down to shield a few kids. He would have shot the perpetrator, provided, of course, that one of the teachers didn't beat him to it.

I have no doubt the staff in my high school was much better armed than the staff of my grammar school across the street. There, too, there was never any occasion for any of the staff to use the weapons they carried. I'm sure the staff of the schools in the small town I grew up in was no different than staff members of other schools. The news in those days was not full of incidents of violence at schools, but school staff members understood it was their responsibility to protect the kids they were charged with from any threat, outside or internal. A gun is one tool that may at any time be needed to provide that protection.

Schools are not the only place in our modern times where crazy people with guns take advantage of unarmed, responsible, law-abiding citizens. The news these days is full of examples. The reason responsible, law-abiding citizens are no longer carrying guns is found in the law-abiding part of the term used. Gun control laws have been enacted to make it illegal to carry a concealed weapon.

Some states, after making it illegal to carry a concealed weapon, offer concealed weapons permits to responsible citizens who meet the state's requirements for carrying a concealed weapon. However, even with a concealed weapon permit, it is still illegal to carry a weapon into the post office, through an airport, into schools, and so many other places that most responsible gun owners have decided it is easier to just leave their gun at home. After all, many responsible gun owners have carried a weapon for years with never a hint of needing it, so why not leave it home?

Was the Second Amendment enacted to give responsible citizens the ability to protect themselves from their irresponsible dangerous countrymen? No! Neither was it enacted by our forefathers to give us the ability to hunt for food. To understand the reason the Second Amendment was enacted, we need to look at what was happening prior to the establishment of our sovereignty.

The English citizens living in America were plagued with unfair treatment by an uncaring government. Right or wrong, these citizens took up their arms and broke free of the oppressive government. With their plight fresh in their minds, they set down on paper the laws that would govern them and their posterity. Chief among the established rights in the new governing documents was the right of free speech followed directly by the right to bear arms for the establishment of a militia that could stand up to a corrupt government that sought to take away the rights of the citizens.

Many years ago, gun laws were established that curtailed one of the most valuable weapons the average citizen could individually handle, fully automatic weapons. At the time, automatic weapons were being used by organized crime to kill not only their competition but also many innocent bystanders. The law made perfect sense and has never really been challenged on the grounds it should have been. Now the only ones with automatic weapons are the government forces, organized crime, and those few citizens that qualify to legally have them and have paid the taxes and fees required to acquire the needed government permits.

As stated above, more recent laws have put further restrictions on gun ownership and possession. The results of which are that the predominant carriers of personal weapons are government forces, organized crime, crazy people, and petty criminals; law-abiding citizens have to worry about too many laws that can be broken while they are carrying their gun. What if they need to stop by the post office?

Gun owners leaving their guns at home has devolved into the deaths of many innocent civilians who only a few decades ago would have had at the ready the means to defend themselves and those around them. At each new outrage of innocent lives lost, our lawmakers advise new gun control laws. Not one of them seems to realize that it was their gun control laws that set the stage in the first place.

The real cure to our problems with gun violence doesn't involve guns at all. It involves care for the mentally deficient that doesn't require the mentally deficient to go out and get a job to pay for their care. It involves police forces that eliminate crime instead of just documenting it. It involves relieving the pressures of too little money and too much need for it. It involves the accepted practice of maintaining a percentage of unemployed citizens to improve the bottom line of business. It involves fixing many of the contemporary problems addressed in this book.

A word of warning: our politicians are out to get our guns because they are in the process of creating the very government our forefathers feared. The gun laws and the situations they have created pave the way for the elimination of citizen-owned firearms. The politicians got the fully automatic weapons. Now they are going for the assault rifles and high-capacity magazines. They are trying to make it look like our right to bear arms is based on our desire to hunt—desire because it is no longer a need—and since handguns are generally not used for hunting, they are in serious jeopardy. The next step is merely a matter of slowly closing parcels of land to hunting until there is very little left, and then the hunting weapons can be taken because there will be no need for them.

Once we see our rights under the Second Amendment eliminated, the elimination of our First Amendment rights can be stepped up. They are already under fire. Regularly we see big news about how the government's hands are tied when it comes to controlling violent video games because the developers and distributors have the right to free expression. Has anyone heard the news about the laws against speaking out against the food industry in Colorado? In Colorado, you can go to jail if you tell anyone about the millions of lives the food industry is taking every year. There is little or no news about it because it is part of the act of taking away our First Amendment rights. The big news stories are the ones that set the stage for giving reason to the elimination of our rights, such as the news about guns and their misuse.

One thing we can all be sure of is that the guns will be long gone before anyone broaches the subject of eliminating our right to vote. That is, other than the one vote that has been denied us from the beginning, our ability to vote for the president. That right was never given because the true leaders of our country, the ones with the majority of the money, wanted to maintain that vote for themselves. We thought we outsmarted the rich by creating term limits for the president, but all we accomplished was the need for the rich to spend more of their money on congressional elections and lobbyists in order to maintain their control of the government.

Does anyone really believe that a law that says you can't have a gun will influence the people who ignore the law against murder?

CHAPTER 25

OUR REPRESENTATIVES

There are many ideas about to be presented in this book that can make this country a better place to live for the majority of Americans. Many of my ideas, however, need close scrutiny by people who care about the majority. To have representatives who care about the majority of America's citizens we must pick them from among the majority. The majority of Americans don't have the funds to run for office. Fortunately we are still the majority, and even if we don't have much money, we can still control the vote.

At the bottom of every list of candidates on a ballot there is a space for "Write-in." Placing Mickey Mouse in this space is very funny, but if we're not careful, we may someday inadvertently elect him. It would be much more advisable to write in a working-class person from among the majority that is smart enough to tell a lawyer what he or she wants, and know when the employee-lawyer delivers it.

What if every person who felt he or she would make a good representative of the people bought a one-dollar ping-pong ball imprinted with his or her name and some sort of positive ID? And what if the named balls were placed in a cage for the district in which the purchaser has lived for the past twenty years? And what if the cages containing the balls for each district were each spun and one ball alone at random was taken out of each cage? The person named on each of the selected balls would probably be a better representative of the majority of the people in that district than any representative they have previously elected.

If the winner of the ping-pong election was known by the majority of the voters in each district, and enough of the voters wrote in the name of the winner of the ping-pong election for their district, then the ping-pong election winner would be the winner in the general election as well.

The key is to be sure that a clear majority of the people in each district have the same name to write in.

CHAPTER 26

TWO-PARTY SYSTEM

Presently our elections come down to two viable candidates for each elected position. One is the Republican candidate and the other is the Democrat candidate. Setting aside the infighting between the Republicans and Democrats, which has made the two-party system laughable, it is ludicrous to assume there are only two viable candidates for each elected position. In fact, for any given position there are literally thousands of suitable Americans that could very effectively fulfill the duties of the given elected office.

CHAPTER 27

PUBLIC PARTICIPATION IN GOVERNMENT

You can't have a government of the people if the people don't participate!

Because it takes millions of dollars to get elected, probably not one representative in the House of Representatives has ever lived payday to payday. Our representatives come from the portion of the population that runs businesses and lays off workers when business is slow in order to preserve profits. They cannot begin to understand what it feels like to have the credit cards maxed out, no savings in the bank, and a paycheck that is so small that you are forced to decide whether to put food on the table or fix the broken car so you can get to work.

How can a person truly represent another when he has no idea what it is like to walk in the other's shoes? If a person from the working class was to magically appear in Congress and stay for twenty years, the majority of that time would be spent in forgetful ignorance of what it is truly like to be one of the working class. Therefore, it is not only important to place people that are truly representative of the population into office but to replace them regularly.

Our representatives and senators divide their time between Washington, DC, and their home states. They strive to keep lines of communications open between themselves and their constituents. The intent is to gain an understanding of what is needed by those they represent. Letters, phone calls, and even face-to-face communications, however, are a poor substitute for actually living the life of those you represent.

I submit that a Representative from the working class could go to Washington, stay there for one or two terms, do the job as he or she sees fit, return home only for vacations, never communicate with his or her constituents, and still never stray from the desires of those represented. I don't condone the idea that representatives, once elected, should isolate themselves from those they represent. I am merely saying they could and still be more effective than those that now represent us.

Finding a way to elect government officials without the need for them to spend money in the process as well as ensuring they are able to continue supporting themselves and their family during the process is only part of what is needed. We also need people who are willing to leave their normal way of life and step into the unknown of public office. The idea of being a senator or a representative has occurred to many if not all of us, but to actually step out there and do it is another matter all together. It is hard enough to get people to vote.

Those with the most life experience would make the best representatives. For this reason and others, it would be best if those that volunteered to run were at the end of their working years and eligible for if not already entered into retirement.

We, the 97 percent of the population that collectively control less money than the remaining 3 percent, have control of the vote. The 3 percent with control of the most money presently control who is on the ballet. "Write In _____," found at the bottom of the list of candidates, is how we can exercise our control. Once common people control Congress, they can enact term limits and official campaign rules that require no money. The next chapter discusses some ideas about how that can be accomplished.

Getting control of the Senate and the House of Representatives in Washington, DC, is the first step. If lotteries for election don't set well with the voters of a district, then another path toward majority rule is to use our social groups such as the PTA, Lions, Elks, Eagles, Masons, Kiwanis, etc. as a platform from which to address an audience of local citizens and tell them why the speaker would be a good choice to represent the voters in their district. Prospective candidates can travel to each of the social group open houses in their district and tell their story. The process can include permission by the participants to allow each of the groups to do a background check.

I'm sure there is no shortage of those that can effectively represent us in Washington, DC, but we need them to participate, or we are doomed to government as usual, which is to say a government in which big business and the rich are the only ones represented.

Majority rule is the basis of democracy. Majority, in this context, is supposed to refer to people. Unfortunately, in present day American democracy it is a minority of the population that rules through having a majority of the money. The only hope the majority of the population has of exercising its intended control is to use its massive number of votes to defeat candidates who spend millions on their campaigns.

This approach will get the attention of those who now spend millions on campaigns but to no avail for them because with common people in public office, people who really know what it is like to live in America, we can make the changes needed to elect our representatives without the need of campaign funds as well as to create term limits.

Common people are the ones that will give us term limits, which will prevent elected officials from staying in office long enough to forget the people they are there to represent. Common people will create an electoral system that doesn't allow elected officials to be forced into submission by those that offer campaign funds. Most importantly, common people as elected officials will pass legislation that is beneficial to the majority of the population.

CHAPTER 28

FREE ELECTIONS

Declaring oneself to be a candidate should be the first step in a free election process. The declaration would be made by filling out an application either online or at the local election office. The application could be submitted anytime after the previous election and no later than six months prior to the primary election in which the candidate intends to run.

The application could begin with the position sought and be followed by pertinent and detailed personal information, including where and when the candidate received his or her education as well as how much education was acquired, every place of employment, length of time the job was held, start and end date, address and phone number of employer, and job or jobs held, the names of coworkers as well as supervisors along with any of their known addresses or phone numbers from each place of employment—any elected positions previously held will be included as previous employment.

An investigator could review the completed application and then use the information given to begin an in-depth investigation into the history of the candidate. The investigator's first step would be to ascertain the validity of all information given on the application. Once the information is verified, the investigator could continue the investigation using not only the information given but by also finding and following every lead possible, including income tax records and any and all public information.

In the course of the investigation, the investigator will uncover a great deal more potential references in the form of friends, family, and acquaintances of the candidate from various points in his or her life. To arrive at a complete and unbiased history of the candidate's life, several investigators may perform simultaneous investigations.

Undoubtedly many people will choose not to run for office in order to avoid such an invasion of their privacy. This desire for privacy is understandable but hardly acceptable for any public official. At least with a full, impartial investigation the facts given will be true and correct as opposed to the present practice of smear tactics, which can neither be trusted nor believed in their entirety.

Every candidate will be given the results of his or her investigation before any publication of the history is made. The candidate, after reviewing the finding, can decide if he or she wishes to continue as a candidate and let that history become public information or withdraw from the candidacy. Once the decision is made to carry on with his or her candidacy, the candidate will be given the opportunity to present orally, in front of a camera, as well as in writing, his or her ideas of what makes him or her the best candidate for office, including what they intend to do if elected.

A candidate's package should contain a complete, verified application, a compiled history of the candidate's life, a written statement provided by the candidate that states his or her beliefs as well as his or her intentions for public office, and a video of the candidate. The package, once completed, should be made available online for review by the voters. To accommodate those voters who are without computer access, anyone wishing to have a paper copy of any or all the packages need only ask to have it sent to the address listed on their voter registration. A DVD of the candidate's video should accompany the paper copy.

A primary election should be held between all the self-nominated candidates. The top ten or possibly twenty candidates for each office should continue on to the main election.

The described process for electing candidates would enable any eligible citizen to run for public office without the need to expend any funds. The voters would be offered the best possible insight into each of the candidates. There would be little or no opportunity within the process for one candidate to use smear tactics on another. The voter would be making his or her decision with factual, proven information.

Candidates with money or financial support could still resort to the current tactics of smearing their opponents. However, any information detrimental to a candidate will probably already have been uncovered by the investigators and be used by the candidate to make the decision to withdraw his or her nomination for office. Furthermore, the voters are sick of the lies and smear tactics of political campaigns, so any attempt to make use of these tactics will probably backfire.

CHAPTER 29

DEMOCRACY

Democracy: A government by the people. Rule of the majority. A government in which the power is vested in the people. These short definitions are some of what you will find if you look up democracy in a dictionary. By its very definition, it should be obvious that without the participation of the people there is no democracy.

Participation begins with voting, but it doesn't end there. In order to have representation, the representatives must have the same roots as the voters they represent. Those roots must go deep and must not have been long out of the ground. Once a person leaves his roots, he or she begins to lose touch. Even if the memories are never lost, the connection is weakened. New connections are made and new roots begin to form.

Presently, without term limits, new representatives, upon their arrival in Washington, are greeted by their multiterm colleagues then taken in hand and shown how things are done before they are allowed to express any of the new ideas they have brought with them. By the time they become full members of the representative body and are allowed to act, they have set aside their new ideas and joined the work in progress, which is no progress and business as usual.

In order to have a true representation in Washington, we must first sweep away the stale incumbents who have no understanding of the people they represent. As we sweep them away, we must replace them with people that are a true representation of the people they serve. Since we are not all lawyers, it hardly makes sense to send a bunch of lawyers to Washington to represent us.

Laws should be written by the people who must live by them. Our representatives in Washington should employ lawyers to look over new bills before they are enacted into law to be sure the bills are properly written and have no loopholes. However, the staff lawyers should be kept subservient to our elected representatives.

Laws should be simple and direct. Anyone should be able to pick up a proposed law, read it, and understand it. We shouldn't need a lawyer to help us understand the laws by which we must live. Lawyers have their place. As pointed out, we need them to make sure the wording is legally correct and carries the meaning we intend it to. No one knows all the laws in existence. Lawyers are trained to find the laws applicable to a situation. Letting lawyers write our laws for us creates a system of government that no one but the most savvy of lawyers can understand.

The use of riders should be eliminated. Presently we have what is call a good old boy system where our representatives vote for bills not because they agree with the content but because they have made an agreement. I'll vote for your bill if you vote for mine. I'll vote for your bill if you let me add this rider to it—the rider often having nothing to do with the original intent of the bill.

CHAPTER 30

SMALL GOVERNMENT?

Politicians, responding to demands from those who contribute to their campaigns, regularly spout the need for smaller government in an effort to gain public support of the idea. We have allowed the wealthy, which make up approximately 3 percent of our population, to seize control of our government and use it to their own benefit. If we allow them to make the government smaller, as they claim we need to do, then the services that will no longer be available for free from a smaller government will be made available by big businesses.

Take a minute to consider what larger government could mean:

Public schools in which class sizes are limited to the optimum size for subject matter and student abilities: Schools that provide education for our children from preschool all the way through to PhD if the student can make the grade. Every child needs to make it through high school just to function in our complicated world, and those who are smart enough and dedicated enough to make it through higher levels of education should be given the opportunity at no monetary cost to them or their families. Presently we are selling opportunity to those with the means to pay while we refuse higher education to those who cannot pay. In the process, we end up with doctors that care more about the money they can make than they do about the patients that seek treatment for sickness and injury. We also have a system of education at the higher levels that cares more about how much money the school can make off its students than it does about giving its students the best education possible. Presently our money-hungry schools of higher education prefer foreign students to domestic students because foreign student pay higher tuition.

Free medical care for the sick and injured. Sickness may be avoided by better nutrition, and injury may be avoided by better safety measures, but no one purposefully gets sick or injured so he or she can receive medical treatment. So why do we attach a monetary cost to people who are already paying with their pain and suffering?

Free mental care would get people off the streets that are a danger to themselves and others. How can a person whose mental condition makes it impossible for him or her to maintain a job pay for needed mental care?

Free dental care to whatever degree is needed from cleaning and a checkup to dental implants where required.

Free medications with research and development done in government labs where profit is not a motive. We have a whole generation of doctors that are trained to be pill pushers because administering pills is directly profitable from the sale and indirectly profitable when the patient needs treatment for side effects.

Free medical transport for emergency treatment as well as for those who just need a ride because their age (young or old), their physical condition (injury, blind), or mental condition (impaired by prescribed narcotic drugs) precludes them from driving.

No medical insurance, which at present redistributes money meant for medical care to those who have nothing to do with the process of caring for the sick and injured and at the same time gives people who know nothing about medicine the right to make the determination as to what medical care an individual will receive.

Better roads on which to drive without the corresponding distribution of tax dollars to people who physically provide no labor toward the building or maintenance of roads.

Bicycle roads separate from motor vehicle roads on which people can safely commute without using finite energy resources and can exercise their bodies in the process. These roads could even be provided with a cover to provide protection from the elements for the riders as well as the roadway.

Free public transportation to further conserve finite energy reserves as well as relieve crowding on our roadways.

Free job training to help make the transition from student to worker.

Free job placement to help put workers and employers together. The employment centers can also place workers into government employment, temporary or permanent, when civilian employers have no present need for new workers.

Free day care available twenty-four hours a day to ensure shift workers have adequate access to safe care for their children. This care could be provided at a center or in a home, depending on need and availability of day-care providers.

Free youth centers to ensure every child has a safe place to go where he or she can meet friends, play organized games, or just hang out.

Free senior centers where adults can get together, meet friends, play organized games, or just hang out.

Free home help for the sick and elderly.

Free legal assistance for everyone, not just criminals. Sometimes we need help to understand and work within our laws. Corporations that have unlimited legal resources are able to financially destroy and thereby prevail over individuals because the individual cannot afford the representation needed to ensure his or her rights are not violated. Everyone should be able to execute a will without regard to how much money they have available to pay a lawyer. We are expected to live within our complicated legal system.

We need to have the right to free legal advice that helps us understand that system.

Well-maintained hiking trails and campsites where people can be close to nature and spend their free time without expense. Building and maintaining trails and campsites provides an opportunity to expend temporary manpower.

Fully manned disaster response forces such as police and fire, as well as major disaster response teams: Presently all of our police and fire services are operating on partial manpower because of a lack of available tax dollars with which to pay them, and there is no trained major disaster force because there is no funding to provide one.

Emergency housing for those displaced by disaster or impending disaster. Sports stadiums just don't fit the bill!

Better protection of our borders.

Full employment at a living wage.

The list above shows some of the ways big government could be beneficial to the majority of the people in this country. The real cost of small government will be taken from the pockets of the 97 percent of the population that controls the smaller portion of the country's wealth in the form of payment for services.

The monetary cost of big government can be taken from the 3 percent of the population that controls the greater portion of the country's wealth while the 97 percent of the population that controls the smaller portion of the country's wealth contributes their labor (only when and as they choose and in return for no less than a living wage) to the operation of the government.

CHAPTER 31

GOVERNMENT LABOR

Government labor can be calculated and quantified to figure its worth and then that value in dollars can be deposited to a special fund within the national treasury that can only be used to pay for government labor and retirement.

The process of calculating and quantifying the value of government labor begins with the simple calculation of what the average rate of pay would be for the particular job, ensuring the pay is at least high enough to comfortably support the worker.

The more difficult task is the quantification. This process figures the value of the particular labor to the country. The value to the country is then divided by the hourly rate of the worker. The final quantification would be expressed as a factor to be multiplied by the hourly wage or biweekly salary of the government worker. The factor times the earned income of each government worker would be added to the special account within the national treasury. The factor would be a constant for each profession, but the rate of pay would vary with the experience level of the worker.

The factors are intended to account for the difference between the value of labor and the dollars paid for the performance of the labor. Federal buildings constructed with government labor, for example, have a definite value—much more value than the cost of the materials that go into constructing the buildings.

The value of the labor used to bring a building into existence can be determined by subtracting the value of the construction materials from the assessed value of the completed building. The process of finding the labor factor would begin by dividing the total value of the labor by the actual cost of the labor. Completing the process would entail evaluating a number of buildings of differing uses.

Construction labor value is pretty straightforward and therefore easily understood and figured. Factors for the labor value of other jobs and professions may not be so easily figured. However, where there is a value, it can be found and figured. It will take a committee, the members of which should include, among others, representatives of the job being evaluated as well as accountants and economists.

The committees are sure to find jobs within the federal government that, although they are worthwhile and important, have no measurable economic value to the country. The quantification of these jobs will likely result in the assignment of a factor of zero or close to it. This is where the special account within the national treasury will come into play. The jobs that have measurable economic value will be placing their full value into the account while removing only their wages or salaries from it. This will leave funds available to pay for some and maybe all of the jobs that are unable to place funds into the account. The net effect will be that federally paid labor will have less and possibly no tax drain on the economy.

The federal government of the United States of America is sovereign. That is to say that there is no entity, with the exception of God, that is in power above them. As such they, or rather, we the people, collectively have the right to say what gives value to the dollars the government prints. Inflation will not be a result of printing money backed by the value of government labor because the wages and salaries of government workers enter the economy at the bottom. Once the money floats to the top of the economy, the excess can be skimmed off like cream floating to the surface of milk. The government will not only in time be able to eliminate the national debt but create a national surplus with which a balanced economy can be maintained.

Full employment is just a step away once we start partially backing the US dollar with federal government labor. There's a plethora of jobs and projects that could be taken up by the federal sector, all of which would benefit the citizens of our country. Many of these jobs and projects are covered in my book *The Service*. Excess workers from the private sector can be employed, with federal funds backed by their labor, to accomplish discretionary projects such as building and operating senior centers and youth centers. Jobs that are common to every town, city, county, and state across America, such as police, firefighters, and teachers can join the federal payroll, where their labor will pay for itself, allowing these agencies to become fully manned. In our schools, class size could be limited to a maximum of fifteen students—less if the students have special needs or the subject matter is extremely difficult. This, of course, would demand the building of more schools and more jobs filled by government workers whose labor pays for itself.

The labor of a federally funded health care system, which is free to those in need of its services, can be fully funded without a corresponding drain on the economy through taxation. This opens the door to a successful socialized medical system and an elimination of the totally flawed health insurance system. There may be a great deal of resistance to this idea by the capitalist medical industry, which puts more emphasis on profits than it does on the well-being of its patients. A large part of their argument might be fingers pointed at the problems of existing socialized medical systems throughout the world. The difficulty with these systems at present is the cost, which must be extracted from the economy, versus the needs of the sick and injured. Virtually free labor would eliminate most of this problem. The remaining cost of materials, such as medical supplies and equipment as well as the materials to build medical facilities, would be far less than the present cost of medical insurance, which is predominantly profits to people who have no direct involvement with medical care.

Pharmaceutical research done in government facilities by federally paid employees can put an end to the enormously wealthy pharmaceutical companies that now control our government agencies and medical schools to their financial benefit and our detriment.

The federal government can offer jobs and a place to work to individuals that suggest a research subject instead of granting them dollars from collected taxes to build their own buildings and pay themselves whatever salary they feel they deserve. The labor, of course, will pay for itself, and the facility can be built using labor that pays for itself. The equipment needed for research and the materials needed to provide a building will be far less of a drain on taxpayer dollars than a grant that includes a massive paycheck for the administrator.

A living wage for every worker will eliminate the need to pay tax dollars in the form of subsidies to private businesses in an attempt to bring the price of their products down to a price lower than its actual cost.

Unemployment insurance payments and welfare payments can be eliminated from the drain on the taxpayers by ensuring that everyone who wants a job can have a job. Jesus said, "The poor will always be with you, and you can help them any time you want." Mark 14:7. Poorhouses can be built, using government labor, to provide room and board for those who are too lazy to work. Our free medical care system should include housing in institutions or on campuses built and staffed for the benefit of those who are mentally or physically incapable of working.

Full employment is a dream for the working class and a nightmare for employers. Imagine how terrible it would be if employers had to entice workers with good working conditions, respect, and a living wage. A word of warning to workers, demanding more than an employer can afford will not get you a better living but rather the loss of whatever the employer's business used to provide before it was forced out of business by its greedy employees. Mutual respect between employer and employee, along with cooperative working relations, is more important than extra money because it can make going to work each day a pleasure instead of a dread. This may at first sound idealistic, but the reality is that working-class people, like it or not, are going to spend a major portion of their waking hours for a major portion of their lives at work, so it is best they enjoy the time they spend at work.

CHAPTER 32

FINANCING GOVERNMENT

There are three ways in which a government can finance its operations. The one we are all most familiar with is taxation. Another is borrowing, in the form of selling government bonds. This one is of great interest and concern as we watch the national debt soar to new heights. The last is seldom addressed and may not readily come to mind. In fact, if it wasn't for the recent hype over the national debt, the average person, if asked how the government finances its operations, would answer with taxes alone.

The third option our government has for paying for its operations is by simply printing money. This option, however, is inflationary whenever it is used without a corresponding increase in national value. Therefore, it would only be appropriate to print money when the printed money can be used to pay for something that will increase the value of the country or when the value of the country has been increased and the supply of money is inadequate to account for the increase.

To illustrate one way the value of the country could be increased, I will use a comparison between the country and a barren piece of property. If a house is built on the, heretofore-barren piece of property, the value of the property has been increased. Similarly, if a new school is built in the United States, then the value of the United States has been increased. Granted, compared to the overall value of the United States, the school equates to a very small increase in the value of the country, but however small, the increase to the country's value cannot be denied.

To illustrate another example, let's say we have two duplicate pieces of property similar in every way but one. One piece of property is located in the State of Spontaneous Combustion. Every building built on this property catches fire and burns to the ground the instant it is completed. The other piece of property is located in the State of Safety, where no building ever built on this property ever burns. Which of the two pieces of property would be more valuable, the one located in Safety or the one located in Spontaneous Combustion? The answer is obvious, and even though these properties don't exist in reality, the reality is that a country with adequate fire protection has more value than a country without it.

Again, let's say we have two duplicate pieces of property similar in every way but one. One piece of property is located in the State of Chaos. On this piece of property everyone who ventures out alone is assaulted. The other piece of property is again located in the State of Safety. No one is ever assaulted on this piece of property. Again, the property located in Safety would be more valuable. Similarly a country with good police protection for its citizens is more valuable than a country with inadequate protection or, worse, a corrupt police force.

Let's compare a country with a highly educated population and one with an illiterate population. Even if the country with an illiterate population has more natural resources within its borders, it is still the poorer nation because an intelligent, well-educated population will find more ways to exploit the resources at its disposal.

These are just a few of the ways a country can increase its value. All of them take manpower to achieve, and some take material resources. If we simply print the money to pay the teachers that educate our population, the craftsmen that build our government buildings, the police and firemen that keep us safe, and the other government workers that make our country more valuable, and then collect taxes to pay for the material resources needed by these people to do their jobs, which increase the value of our country, then the increase in the country's value is going to be greater than the amount of money printed, and there will be no inflation caused by the printing of the money.

Without bothering with humorous analogies, let's agree that a country with free exceptional medical care for its population is more valuable than a country with a mediocre medical care system that preys on its population for the funding to operate the system while paying high profits to investors and insurance companies. The funds to pay the doctors their exorbitant salaries as well as the wages of every other worker associated with the free medical system could safely be paid with printed dollars without fear of inflation. The medical equipment to furnish the medical centers and hospitals shouldn't be purchased with printed funds. They must be purchased with taxed dollars because the equipment is produced by private industry and includes profits that can be inflationary when they are paid with printed funds that may seem to be of a never-ending supply to those who spend them, and especially to those who receive them.

Beyond the reasoning that it is fiscally safe to print money for labor that adds value to the country, there is the added factor that all the funds paid to labor directly contribute to consumer spending, which is the foundation on which a nation's economy rests. Another safeguard is that the dispensing of printed funds for expended labor alone places a control on the amount of money printed. In other words, every dollar printed is backed by expended labor.

In the event the money supply grows too fast, the resulting excess money will be found at the top of the economy, where all spent funds eventually arrive. The simple fix is to tax the excess money back into the government coffers, where it can be safely stored until it is needed by a rapidly expanding economy or a massive public need such as in the case of a natural disaster.

Taxes, the first of the three forms of financing government operations, should as much as possible be collected from the top of the economy, where the money has already fulfilled its intended purpose.

Taking money from the bottom of the economy, or, if you will, its foundation—in other words, the pockets of the working class—does damage to the economy by reducing consumer spending. This is best illustrated by tracking the path of money from the pockets of the working class to the pockets of the rich individuals and businesses at the top of the economy.

The largest portion of a working class person's income is spent on housing. If he or she owns a house, then the major portion of the monthly house payment is interest that goes to a bank, where a portion of the paid interest pays for the operation of the bank, the upkeep of the bank's buildings, and the wages and salaries of the bank's employees. Most of the interest, however, goes directly to the top of the economy. If a family rents their house from an individual, then the rent payment goes to the individual that owns the house, the landlord. If the landlord still owes money on the house, then the rent payment is probably mostly a referred house payment with a little left over to pay for house maintenance and may include some living capital for the landlord. If the landlord owns the house outright, then the rent payment adds to the landlord's income. In some cases the rent payment may be the retired landlord's entire income. Many renters live in apartments, and most apartment complexes are corporate owned, so most of the rent flows to the top of the economy while a small portion of it pays for the maintenance of the apartment building and the wages of the workers that manage and maintain the apartments.

Houses and apartments alike require utilities. The portion of the worker's wages paid to utilities fund the upkeep of the utilities equipment and distribution system. It pays the employee wages and salaries and funds the purchase of the utility company vehicles as well as maintenance and fuel for the vehicles. Most utilities are corporate owned, so the portion of the utility payment that is not needed to fund the operation of the utility flows to the top of the economy.

Most working class people need a car to carry out their daily routines. The purchase of a new car helps support the dealer that sold the car and all of the dealer's employees as well as the manufacturer of the car and all the manufacturer's employees, but it doesn't stop there because the suppliers of the parts and raw materials that go into the car also have employees. The employees of all the aforementioned, businesses are not the only ones paid by the purchase of a new car. What about the buildings that house all these businesses and the craftsman that built them? Even with all the things the money paid to purchase a car supports, a very large portion of the money spent still goes directly into the corporate coffers at the top of the economy.

Everyone needs to eat, but for the working class food costs eat up a larger percentage of their income. Money spent at the grocery store pays the wages of all the employees working there, but their jobs are not the only ones supported by the purchase of groceries. The farm workers, who are now mostly employees of agricultural corporations, receive a trickle of the money spent on groceries, as do the employees that maintain the farm equipment. The truck drivers that move the crops from the fields to the factories, from the factories to the warehouses, and from the warehouses to the stores get their share, as do the mechanics that maintain the trucks. The flow of money from the grocery consumer's pocket doesn't stop there because someone has to sell the farm equipment and the trucks that move food products. Of course, the trucks and equipment cannot be sold until they are made, and someone has to build them.

There is a long list of workers whose livelihood depends on the purchases of other workers, and for the hundreds of dollars that are paid to workers, thousands of dollars are sent directly to the top of the economy, where they are invested in the pursuit of more dollars. They are invested in things such as government bonds that create the national debt and pay interest to the investors. The smart thing for our elected officials to do is tax this money, which has been extracted from the general economy, instead of borrowing it and paying interest on it, but the holders of this pot of money use a great deal of it to pay for campaign contributions and lobbying. So the voters are told it is best not to tax the pot of money because it is this pot of money that creates jobs and pays the workers' wages, when in truth it is the other way around—the wages of the working class people pay the salaries and wages of other working people as the money rises through the economy on its way to building the pot of money at the top of the economy.

The government is not the only one that borrows from the pot of money found at the top of the economy. Most workers use credit cards because so much of their paycheck is taken in taxes, interest, and insurance that they haven't enough left to make it from one payday to the next. The stores receive their payment from the pot when the credit cards are used to make a purchase, and the worker is left with even more interest to pay out of the next check.

Houses are also paid for out of this pot, and the occupant spends the greater part of the rest of his or her life depositing interest into the pot to cover the massively inflated cost of the house. The inflated house price is not a result of an inflated economy but rather a manipulation by the holders of the pot.

The voters need to demand free elections so that the elected officials are no longer beholden to campaign contributors. We will know we have finally achieved a government of the people when we see tax dollars coming from the pot that rests on top of the economy, which is only accessible to a select few, instead of coming from the pockets of the working class, who are already tasked with supporting the economy with their paychecks (consumer spending).

A major expense for all working class families is insurance—car, house, life, medical—and the majority of each payment goes directly to the top of the economy. The more you look at where the working class spend their money, the more obvious it is their paychecks are the foundation on which the economy rests. The money spent will all eventually rise to the top of the economy, and that is where it should be skimmed off and used to support the operations of the government.

To have a strong economy, it is essential that personal debt be eliminated, everyone who wants or needs a job is employed, and every employee be paid a living wage that includes a surplus for savings.

To have a strong nation, it is essential to pay off the national debt and finance the operations of government predominantly by the collection of taxes. Printing money can help the nation, as well as its economy, grow stronger as long as it is balanced with a corresponding increase in value. Borrowing money should be eliminated as a source of funds by creating a surplus in the government coffers, in the same way that individuals should save for large purchases and unexpected expenses.

The national debt should be stopped by the elimination of borrowing and paid off through the collection of taxes. The government should regularly dig deep into the pot resting on top of the economy, taking out enough money to run the government, place some money in reserve (a savings account), and regularly pay off some of the outstanding government bonds until they are all retired.

CHAPTER 33

PAYING FOR MILITARY MANPOWER

To quantify and calculate the value of a soldier's labor we must, like any other job, consider what he or she provides. Death and destruction immediately come to mind. It could be argued that soldiers keep the country safe, and to a degree this is true. Having spent the bulk of my life working for the military, I would like nothing more than to believe this wholeheartedly, but the fact is that when a soldier goes to work, his focus is on death and destruction. Granted that when he does his job in another country the death and destruction are not felt at home, but he most definitely is inviting the death and destruction to be sent to his home. Soldiers are needed, and their service is most important when they defend their home turf, but as they do their defending, the death and destruction inevitably includes the civilians the soldier is being paid to protect. Using the heretofore discussion, the only possible factor of the quantifying and calculating process is going to be a negative number. Determining how large that negative number is would require the specifics of a large number of actual engagements. The total loss of each engagement could be divided by the total number of soldiers involved, and a factor could be established by averaging all the engagements selected for computation.

The proposed simple calculation, however, doesn't take into account the death, destruction, and occupation of homeland prevented by the defensive engagement. Furthermore, there is the simple fact that the mere existence of force a collection of soldiers represents can prevent an invasion from occurring.

Using history as a tool, we can change the direction of this discussion toward a possible resolution. First of all, if we at some point were able to somehow come up with a plausible argument to give the soldier a positive factor, history tells us our rich leaders would undoubtedly cause our nation to regularly engage in military conflict. Conversely, a negative factor could have the same effect because it could cause the excess cost of manning an army to result in a force that is too small to prevent conflict.

Throughout history we have seen that common men do not precipitate military conflict. It is without exception the rich that initiate conflict. The common man is simply sent out to die in the conflict. So the solution might be that only taxes collected on incomes of $1 million or more can be used to finance an army. Of course, it would be important to stipulate the percentage of the millionaires' tax dollars that can be used for purchasing military manpower.

We could continue on with discussions that have so many what ifs that a solution is almost impossible to find, or we could change direction again. Let's finally adopt the government our forefathers envisioned by electing common people to make our national decisions. An important part of electing common people to office is that they don't stay in office long enough to lose their commonality. As stated, common people go off to die in wars; they don't start them. Common people will think long and hard before they send their children off to die in a war. It is plainly seen in history that every war that was ever fought was initiated for financial gain. Common people are not in a position to make financial gains from war. Representatives who come from common life for a short while are likely to engage military forces only for extreme defensive need.

With governments that truly are of the people, we may finally see world peace and have no need of ever engaging military personnel in combat, but we will always need them, and they should always be paid with taxes paid by those they defend.

If you have any doubt about whether we should have American military forces stationed in foreign countries, read *Blowback*, by Chalmers Johnson.

CHAPTER 34

HOUSING

House loans are a plague on private individuals. They easily take up 40 percent of the household income for many working class families. To get away from them as well as the need for them, we need only make it unprofitable for the banks to loan money for private housing.

Without the availability of borrowing to purchase a home, house prices will need to fall to a point where a person can save enough money in a few years to purchase a house in cash. If this seems impossible, take into account what it takes to build a house. The amount of labor one person can expend in one year is more than is needed to build a very big house. The materials required to build the house are included in its price, as is the land. Land is only worth the price someone will pay to purchase it. If the money must be saved for the purchase, that price will not be as high as it is with credit available. The materials needed to build a house are almost all mass-produced. The largest portion of contemporary house prices is profit. Most of this profit goes to the developers that purchase large tracts of land, massive quantities of materials, and then pay workers to put the houses together. Homebuyers of the last thirty to forty years also made huge profits when they became sellers. The houses, without their massive profits, are relatively cheap and should be brought back to a price commensurate with their worth.

CHAPTER 35

A LIVING WAGE

A living wage has been mentioned repeatedly, but how much money must we be paid to say we actually have enough money to live on? A minimum wage has been enforced in various areas of the country, and it varies from area to area, but I have not seen one yet that actually gives the recipient enough money to live on, much less support a family. Instead, the minimum wage is just enough to allow the recipient to qualify for credit, which they then use to supplement the minimum wage in order to live. This, of course, is a trap because when the minimum wage earner doesn't have enough money to live on in the first place and then takes out credit to supplement his or her meager income, at best he or she can only make payments on the debt with no hope of ever paying it off. The following formula takes into account the fact that everyone needs food, shelter, and, although it is not specifically mentioned, clothes. To satisfy these needs, we need to commute to work. There is, of course, more that we need and a great deal more that we want. This formula is designed to satisfy all the needs and some wants in the absence of available debt.

$$\text{Living wage} = \frac{\frac{P}{60} + S + T + \frac{V}{36} + \frac{u}{12} + F}{40 \times 4}$$

Where:

> **H** is equal to the average price of a comfortable three-bedroom house with a yard and garage in a decent neighborhood.
>
> **S** is equal to **H** divided by 60 and accounts for the minimum amount of money that every worker should have available to add to savings every month.
>
> **T** is equal to the average cost of transportation and accounts for the cost of commuting to work for a month, fuel for two vehicles for a month, two nights in a decent hotel, and twenty-four individual meals in a decent restaurant.
>
> **V** is equal to the average cost of a good new family-friendly vehicle.
>
> **U** is equal to the average cost of a good used family-friendly vehicle
>
> **F** is equal to the monthly cost of providing a family of four with three meals a day plus snacks that consist of plant-based whole food that is fresh, raw, and in sufficient quantity to maintain health.

The living wage derived from this formula, if actually used for all the items specifically mentioned, would still leave money available for extra needs that are not mentioned. The actual intent, however, is not to place everyone's needs and wants in a box. Whether or not someone wants to buy a house is irrelevant. He or she still needs money available to pay for a place to live: **H**. However, if he or she does decide to buy a house the person should be able to save the money to buy the house within five years: thus **S**. He or she also needs to have a place to live while saving: **H**. To eliminate the need for house insurance, the person should be able to save enough money to buy another house and then retain the saved money in savings: **S** after purchase. Once you buy a house, you need to maintain it: **H** after purchase.

People need to have vacations in order to maintain sanity as well as just enjoy their life. If you look closely, the money for vacations is built into **T**. **S** can periodically give you an extraordinary vacation, if you so chose, or furnish a house, and eventually some of your other wants.

Not everyone is going to need a new car every three years, but they should have the money to buy one: **V**, and if they decide to use the money elsewhere they should have that choice as well.

Most families need a second car; **U**. They may not need to purchase one every year, but used cars need maintenance: **U**.

Some people want to travel around the world, especially when they are young: **H, S, T, U, F**, no problem.

A young couple who both work can save enough money during a long engagement to start their marriage in a fully paid-for house. Once they decide to have a family, one can work and the other can stay home, or they can both work and have even more money to spend on the family and their combined wants.

Some people may find they can live on less than the income that forty hours of work a week at a living wage can provide. They may choose to work only fifteen hours a week.

A living wage is the minimum pay; most jobs will pay more—greater opportunity to spend more time with the family or acquire those really big wants.

Simply plugging in the living wage at the bottom of the government pay scale and then adjusting the rest of the salaries proportionally upward can modify the general schedule the government now uses for its salaried employees.

For wage grade employees, the living wage can be inserted at the bottom of the pay scale, and the rest of the wages can be adjusted upward.

Private sector employers will need to adjust their wages and salaries to entice workers to work for them instead of the government. The increased buying power of the consumer will make it possible for the private sector employers to make adjustment to their prices in order to pay the increased wages and still stay in business. The period of adjustments between wages and prices may be extremely interesting, but it shouldn't be painful for anyone and should result in a balancing of the economy that can be maintained, possibly indefinitely.

The intent of the living wage is to correct the mistake commonly made by employers who routinely pay their employees such meager wages that there is not enough buying power in the economy to keep the economy operating. The solution of credit is a temporary fix that will always result in an eventual catastrophic collapse of the economy.

The seeming excess pay built into the living wage formula will create the opportunity for the smart worker to save an enormous quantity of money that will protect the worker and his family from unforeseen catastrophic expenses (this eliminates the need of insurance) and allow for major purchases as well as regular family vacations, but, most importantly, the total savings of all workers will provide the banks with adequate funds to finance the formation of the businesses needed to supply the goods and services an economy needs to be viable.

CHAPTER 36

THE PRICE OF FOOD

The price of food must be set high enough to give farmers the incentive to grow the food. Once the price is determined, the government must be prepared to purchase all food produced at the price established to ensure the farmer can make a living at farming. This doesn't mean the government will purchase all the food grown by farmers; it simply means no one will be able to force the farmer to sell his or her crop at a price that doesn't allow the farmer and his family to go on living and farming.

It is becoming evident that the human body functions best on a diet of fresh plant-based whole food. Those who choose to eat differently will find the cost of their food is cheaper. To ensure everyone can afford the food they choose, I am using the lowest yield per crop to establish a baseline. The viruses, chemicals, and radiation used to modify GMO foods create a seed that produces a plant with a higher yield per acre than its heirloom ancestors. Therefore, the baseline will be derived using heirloom seeds. Use of chemical fertilizers, herbicides, and pesticides also increases yield, so the baseline will be established using plants that are grown without the aid of any of these products. Plants need fertile soil in order to reach their full nutrition potential. The baseline will stipulate that a combination of chicken, cow, horse, and pig fertilizer is used. It will further stipulate that the animals that provide the fertilizer are healthy, free roaming, antibiotic free, and eat no GMO food, and the food they do eat is a natural food for them. The baseline will henceforth be referred to as naturally grown.

Here is a formula for determining the price of naturally grown fruits, vegetables, and tree nuts.

$$P = \frac{A}{Y}$$

Where:

P is equal to the unit price for each type of naturally grown fruit, vegetable, or tree nut.

Y is equal to the potential units yielded annually from a twenty-acre field of one type of naturally grown fruit, vegetable, or tree nut.

A is equal to an annual living income.

Annual living income varies from a living wage in two ways. First, it is figured for an annual income instead of an hourly wage, and secondly it doesn't include a cost for food. The exclusion of food is twofold. First, the formulas can't both have a value that changes the other because you will end up with an ever-increasing loop when you try to solve both equations. Second, farmers have the means to feed themselves and their families without significant cost. The formula for an annual living income would be expressed as:

$$A = (L \times 40 \times 52) - (F \times 12)$$

Where:

L is equal to the current living wage,

and

F is equal to the monthly cost of food used to figure the current living wage.

The government will use the formula to establish the price it will pay for all naturally grown fruits, vegetables, and tree nuts. The baseline price the government pays for a particular naturally grown food is the same price at which the government will sell all the particular type food regardless of growing method. In other words an apple that is naturally grown will be purchased at a higher price than a sprayed apple that is grown using chemical fertilizer, herbicides, and pesticides, but both apples will be sold at the same price.

Using this formula to determine the price of produce will enable anyone that can acquire twenty acres of land and who wishes to become a farmer to earn an annual living income from the small farm. Twenty acres is used because a person can work twenty-acres of land without the assistance of machinery or hired help. Guarantee there will be a lot of people who decide the work is more than they're willing to do, but for those who wish to stick it out, they will earn their annual living income in spades. Those who own bigger farms and use machinery may earn a very good living from their toils. Keep in mind that land and equipment is not cheap to buy or maintain, so larger farms will have greater expenses. The farmer may also need help to work their land and the help will demand no less than a Living Wage, and rightfully so.

The starting point for determining a fair price for each type of fruit, vegetable, and tree nut, as previously stated, is to use the yield that can be expected from sowing twenty acres of naturally prepared land with heirloom seeds. A farmer that reaps the expected yield from this planting without the use of pesticides, herbicides, or chemical fertilizers can sell the crop to the Government and receive an annual Living Income.

A farmer growing a similar crop with the use of pesticides, herbicides, chemical fertilizers, or GMO seeds can expect a higher yield per acre. The corresponding price per unit of yield will be lower so that the farmer will still receive an annual living Income from twenty acres.

The Government will sell all its produce at the price it pays for naturally grown produce from heirloom seed. The difference between the price paid for chemically grown and or genetically modified produce will go toward labeling the produce and then tracking and researching any health problems that appear to be associated with the unnatural produce.

The farmer is not locked into producing one crop. In fact, it would be a mistake to plant only one crop. The effect of setting the price of produce based on each crop's expected yield from twenty acres is that any proportion of different crops will still result in an annual living income for the farmer. To illustrate, planting two acres of tomatoes will return 2/20th of an annual living income. A four-acre apple orchard will yield 4/20th of an annual living income. An acre of brussel sprouts will yield 1/20th of an annual living income. Three acres of spinach will yield 3/20th of an annual living income. Five-acres of grapes will yield 5/20th of an annual living income. A three-acre almond orchard will yield 3/20th of an annual living income. Two acres of beets will yield 2/20th of an annual living income. The seven crops collectively add up to 20/20th, which equals 1, or an annual living income.

At harvest time, any farmer that grows fruits, vegetables, or tree nuts, may call the government and request pickers to harvest the crop. The pickers will arrive on the date and time arranged by the farmer, pick the ripe produce, pack it for shipment, and load it on a truck. If the government is purchasing the produce, then it will provide the truck and make payment to the farmer. The pickers will return on subsequent days to pick the produce that wasn't yet ripe on the first harvest. On larger farms, the pickers may set up a camp and stay awhile or have a permanent barracks nearby.

The crops that readily lend themselves to being planted and harvested by machinery make it possible for one farmer to sow and reap a larger harvest. To economically farm these crops takes more land. Therefore, an annual living income for farmers who grow corn, grains, peanuts, dry beans, and most other crops whose yields are generally measured in bushels should be figured on the expected yield of one hundred sixty acres. The baseline for these crops will still be figured using naturally grown plants. The formula to figure these crops will substitute the yield from one hundred sixty acres for the twenty acres used previously.

A farmer that uses chemical pesticides, herbicides, and/or chemical fertilizers and/or GMO seeds will receive less per bushel for his or her crops. The yield per acre of the unnaturally grown crops is generally higher, so the net income will be relatively the same. The price the government sells the crops for will be the same no matter the method of growth.

If a farmer decides to sell his or her crop to the government, then at harvest time government trucks will arrive at the farm. The trucks can be loaded using the farmer's machinery. The crop will be taken to a government storage facility, where it will be available for sale at the price determined for naturally grown food. Unnaturally grown food will be kept separate from naturally grown food, but the sale price will be the same.

The farmer that grows unnatural crops will be able to undersell the government if they choose, but they will be forced to label their product as to how it differs from naturally grown crops in the same way the government labels all produce before sale. That is, the food will be labeled as to where, when, and how the crop was grown, as well as by whom the crop was grown. Any immediate ill effects of the food can instantly be traced back to the farm it came from so that measures can be taken to help the farmer do better with the next crop.

The crops purchased by the government that don't sell right away will be stored if possible for when they are needed. The perishable produce that doesn't readily lend itself to being stored may be used to feed government-owned pigs or some other livestock. The food may also be sold to citizens of other countries. The price the food is sold for out of country needs to be figured for the country in which it is sold. In other words, we need to figure a living wage for that country and then use it to figure The annual living wage income for their farmers, and then price the food so that it sells for the same price for which their farmers will sell it. In that way, we will not be competing with the farmers of other nations but simply supplementing the crops grown by their farmers in order to fill the country's needs.

This means the government will buy food at the US price and sell it at a price that will in all likelihood be cheaper. How can we do this? I'm glad you asked. Crops of produce represent value that has come into existence from virtually nothing, so the money to pay for it need not come from the taxpayer. The money can be printed when necessary and paid to the farmer. The money paid for the produce the government sells to the consumer can go into an account similar to the federal service labor account. For discussion purposes, we can call this account the federal food account. Money that comes out of the federal food account can only be spent to purchase food crops. The printed money will go into the economy through the farmer's pocket. The money used to purchase the food from the government will come out of the economy through the consumer's pocket. The difference in prices will cause the balance in the federal food account to rise and fall. Some of the money will be placed back into the economy through the pockets of other farmers. Some money from the federal food account will be lost in sales to other countries at lower prices. Food that is stored in silos or giant root cellars will represent future income to the federal food account. To make up for sales of food at a loss, stored food, food fed to government livestock, and food served in government dining halls, money will periodically need to be printed to make purchases. The printed money will be placed in the pockets of farmers, from which it will eventually rise to the top of the economy, where a portion and possibly all of it will be taken back out of the economy as taxes.

A safeguard needs to be enacted to ensure our greed doesn't starve the citizens of other countries. A tariff equal to the difference in the computed prices for each crop of differing countries will ensure that only a country's surplus food will be sold. In other words, if an apple is purchased for $2 in the United States, and a farmer in Mexico will sell his apples for fifty cents, then the United States will impose a $1.50 tariff on every apple an American business owner has shipped into the United States from Mexico.

Seed patents have proven to be a bad idea and should be eliminated. The patents were intended to ensure that the developers of new seeds could recover their research and development cost, but instead the developers have seen fit to use nature and the lobbied-for patent law to steal land and unfairly tax farmers through the annual repurchase of seed.

The set price paid by the government is the lowest price anyone will be forced to accept as payment for his or her crop. The farmer may be able to sell the crop for a higher price and may even decide to accept a lower price, but no one will be forced to give up farming because they can't make a living at it.

A living wage that includes the price of food will ensure consumers will be able to purchase food for themselves and their families no matter the cost. Government subsidies that are supposed to reduce the cost of food are ridiculous. They don't ensure people have food to eat. Our current economy demands a certain percentage of unemployment. How cheap do you think you need to make food so that a person who has no income can afford it? Let's try ensuring that everyone who wants a job can have a job that pays a living wage, and then there is no seemingly valid argument for wasting the taxpayers' dollars on subsidies.

GMO crops by law are equivalent to natural crops, but since their inception the number of children affected with food allergies and autisms has exploded. There is no proof that the GMO food is to blame, but then without tracking of the food there couldn't be any concrete proof of cause and effect. GMO foods as well as food grown using chemical fertilizers, pesticides, and herbicides need to be labeled, and special attention needs to be paid to see if we are allowing ourselves and our progeny to be poisoned.

The produce purchased by the government may be served in a government dining hall, or it may be sold to anyone that wants to buy it. The government-purchased produce leaving the farm will travel to a government warehouse. A store may send a truck to the government warehouse to pick up produce to sell. A restaurant, depending on its demand, may bring its truck to the loading dock of the government warehouse or drive its van to the other side of the building and enter the produce store where it can hand pick its produce.

The farm at which the government pickers pick produce may be a twenty-acre farm or a thousand-acre farm, but it may also be a private residence where the homeowner's garden produces more food than the family needs. The government pickers will go anywhere and everywhere there is fresh produce to be picked. They will pick the food, package it for shipment, load it on a truck, and if the owner has no other plan to sell the food, then the government workers will take it away and make it available for purchase as soon as possible so that the consumer daily can get fresh plant-based whole food.

The family that has room for a garden and time to tend it can have the pick of their produce and a small income from their excess. The large lot owner and small landowner can have an opportunity to turn their spare time into extra income while enjoying the fruit of their labor. The farmer, after reaping his crop, may find time on his hands that can be used to work at a job that can furnish him or her with extra income that can make it possible to save money in preparation for the possible future loss of a partial or whole crop or simply to pay for bigger wants.

CHAPTER 37

GOVERNMENT PICKERS

Every American at the age of nineteen years old should enter the service where they will learn to do a job of their choosing and have the opportunity to work at that job until their twenty-second birthday. The exception to this rule will be the pickers. They will be released from their service obligation at the age of twenty-three.

The extra year is needed to ensure the pickers get adequate training for a marketable job. It is unlikely that anyone will choose to be a picker for his or her chosen career. Pickers need to be able-bodied young people. Athletes that do well in high school sports and wish to continue could be adversely affected by the three-year break required to complete their service requirement.

Therefore, one of the service choices available to high school students should be sports. The inductees can choose their sport of choice as their career option, but there's a catch. In the off-season, in addition to training for their sport and training for their alternate job, which we will get to shortly, they must pick crops. They must also sign up for four years of service instead of three. After two years of playing sports, if it is obvious that they will not be picked up by a professional team at the completion of their service commitment, then they need time to retrain.

The alternate job I mentioned is major disaster response personnel. Presently there is no trained force to respond to major man-made or natural disasters. The athletes in pursuit of a professional athletic career who pick crops by hand in their off-season will be trained as hazmat technicians, confined space rescue, firefighters, emergency medical technicians, and a variety of other jobs related to emergency rescue and recovery. The teams will be distributed throughout the nation. Therefore, the players and their emergency equipment will be distributed throughout the nation. In an emergency, a force of whatever size needed can immediately respond from different points of the country to the disaster area. The service personnel will make up the bulk of the manpower for the major emergency response force. The trainers and supervisory personnel for the major emergency response force will come from the members of the force that choose to continue working for the government after their service commitment is complete and from trained fire department personnel who wish to join the major emergency response force.

Pickers who don't take their job seriously can be washed out of picking crops along with their sport. They can choose to learn a totally new job, or they can remain in the major emergency response force, which will become their full-time job for the remainder of their four-year commitment. Similarly, if at the end of two years no professional team scouts show interest in picking him or her for their team, then the athlete can change careers and still have enough time left to be trained, work full time on the major emergency response force, or switch to firefighting for a career.

CHAPTER 38

THE PRICE OF A HOUSE

The cost of a house weighs heavy in the living wage formula because housing costs have inflated to a much higher degree than the general rate of inflation. Using the present housing cost to figure a living wage could easily result in the price of everything else inflating to the same level that the cost of a house has risen. The alternative is to decrease the cost of houses. Either way, the economy will balance and everyone will have enough money to live. The question is do we want to pay ten dollars for an apple?

To build a house, you need a place to put it—the cost of the land. You need the materials to build it—the cost of materials. You need craftsmen to build it—the cost of labor. The three costs— labor, materials, and land— add up to the value of a house to the person who has enough money saved to purchase the land, buy the materials, and pay the craftsmen who built the house. You may argue that I have left out the cost of the permits, which can be phenomenally expensive.

I did, but I submit that charging for permits is counterproductive as well as downright theft. We pay taxes for our city and county governments to operate, and they should charge enough taxes to ensure they can operate without additional charges. The point of getting permits is to let the city and county inspectors know that you are doing something that they should take a look at. If you draw the plans yourself, then they need to look at the plans and ensure the building will stand and stay standing, the electrical and plumbing systems are sound, and everything in the proposed house is up to code. The codes are written as lessons learned from doing things wrong. Placing a price on the permit process takes the focus away from inspections and puts it on an enforcement process centered on collecting money. Special interest groups have lobbied to take responsibilities away from the city and county building departments and to place it on outside agencies that charge for their services. Instead of drawing the plans myself, which I personally am quite able to do; I have to pay an architect to draw the plans and place his stamp on it. Once I bring the plans to the building department, the inspector will take a cursory look, charge me a fee, and go back to drinking his coffee; his job has already been done by another, and I get to pay three times for one disservice.

Taking profits and permit costs out of the cost of a house, we are left with land, materials, and labor. This is the true value of a house. Faithfully using the living wage formula will ensure everyone can afford the price of land, materials, and labor to build a house. If we want to include massive profits for speculators and investors, and we want to maintain the blatantly flawed permit process along with forced purchase of advice, then we can still afford the price of a house, but we'll also see a dramatic increase in the price of everything else we buy in order to pay a living wage to workers.

Either way, as long as we pay the living wage, everyone will be able to afford to live. The advantage of the inflated living wage to match the inflated house price is that we will pay off our personal debts, including houses and the national debt, much sooner.

Once things balance, the cost of materials to build a house, plus the cost of the labor to build a house, plus the cost of land on which to build a house, will equal the price of a house. So if we leave the average price of a comfortable three-bedroom house with a yard and garage in a decent neighborhood at $200,000, and knowing what a living wage equals, then we can get an idea of what the cost of materials to build a house will grow to. If we figure the cost now of the land, materials, and labor it takes to build a house, and use this figure to compute a living wage, then we will see the cost of things balance out pretty much where they are with the exception of the cost of a house, which will drop significantly. As long as we ensure that it is not worthwhile for a bank to loan money for a house or any other consumer need or want, we will see the price of a house drop to the cost of land, labor, and materials because that is what people will pay to build their own house, to their own specifications, based on their available savings. When and if the people who build their own house decide to sell their house, they will have no reason, other than greed to charge more than they paid to build it, and figuring wear and tear they should probably charge less, especially since the buyer can build his or her own new house if he or she chooses.

CHAPTER 39

PRICING A COMMODITY

Labor is the most important payment a business can make. A person who goes into business does so in order to receive an income. The intent is to assure the income is enough to support the owner and his or her family. The worker goes to work to assure he or she has enough money to support himself or herself and his or her family. The intent is the same with both the worker and the owner, and they both have wants that far exceed the support of their families. Many businesses begin with one man or woman and an idea. The business is only viable if the business pays all the bills, including a personal salary that the owner feels is personally acceptable, and is left with a profit.

Once the owner has figured out what all the bills for the business will be, he or she needs to figure out where the bills fit. The bills need to be separated into fixed and variable costs. The cost of raw materials per unit of output is a variable cost to the business because the business only expends the cost of the raw material if it produces a unit of product. The owner's salary and a place to work are fixed costs to the business because they need to be paid no matter how many units of product the business produces. So if the business produces one unit of product, then the price for that unit must at least cover the cost of all the fixed costs plus the variable costs associated with one unit of product plus a profit. For two units the business would add the variable cost associated with the second unit of product to the total costs figured for the first unit produced and divide the result by two.

One unit may be all the business is going to produce. However, if the business is going to produce as many units as possible, then the prospective businessperson needs to have an idea of what that monthly number might be. The owner estimates the number of units that can be made in a month, then multiplies that number by the fixed costs associated with each unit of product and adds the result to the monthly fixed costs of the business. The business needs to make a profit to stay in business, so the desired profit is added in before dividing the entire costs, including the profit, by the expected number of units the business can manufacture in a month. If the price can be borne by the market, then the owner may have the basis for a viable business.

Profit can buy sailboats and racecars, but the business really has no need for sailboats or racecars unless that is the business of the business. Profit first must make up for any units that don't sell. Profits are also needed if the business is ever going to expand—maybe hire an employee or more employees. Keep in mind that the owner who works in the business and employee(s) are both employees. Their pay shouldn't be much different. I don't mean the owner should accept starvation wages; in fact, he or she determined the salary before starting the business. I am also not suggesting the employee demand more wages than his or her skill and time would warrant. The employee's wage, which should never be less than a living wage, was agreed on before employment began. The profits don't really belong to either of the employees, even though one of them is the owner; the profits belong to the business. Granted the owner has the right to say how the business spends its money, but the business's money should be used for everything the business needs before it is spent on the owner's personal wants. In fact, it is best to leave profits in the business to cover future costs, especially of the unexpected nature. The owner should never take anything more than the predetermined salary out of a business before that business has a secure ownership of all assets; that is, no debt and enough money in savings to be secure enough to stay in business or retire the owner if needed. If there is enough money left after all of that is covered, then the owner may choose to proclaim a dividend.

Monthly retained profit is the determining factor in figuring the time frame necessary to attain secure ownership. The price, of course, has to be reasonable before patrons will pay it. The costs underlying price, which are fixed costs, variable costs, and profits, give the business a dollar figure for price, which it can't go below.

Once the business figures its earning potential at the minimum price for the offered commodity, it's time to figure the business's income taxes for the expected income. Income tax should be a fixed cost, which varies with income. The expense for income tax, once figured, is inserted into the fixed costs to make the final computations for a price of commodity below which the business cannot go.

A simple tax structure aids a business in determining a price for its commodity. Tax deductions for business expenses are unnecessary; the business passes on its tax burden in the same way it passes on the cost of everything it buys, in its "price of commodity."

CHAPTER 40

IT'S JUST BUSINESS

There are three main types of business: sole proprietorship, partnership, and corporation. Sole proprietorship is a business owned by one person. The owner and the business are essentially one entity for tax purposes, debt purposes, liability purposes, and pretty much every other purpose. A partnership is a business owned by two or more people. The owners and the business are essentially one entity for tax purposes, debt purposes, liability purposes, and some other but not all purposes. A corporation is a business owned by one or more people. The owners and the business are separate entities for tax purposes, debt purposes, liability purposes, and every other purpose.

There are a variety of corporation types. Business owners decide whether to set up a sole proprietorship, a partnership, or a particular type of corporation based on the benefits to the owner. I submit that a business should always be a separate entity from its owner and should just be "business."

The owner's take from a business, if any, is salary and shows up as a fixed cost to the business. The business's take from a business is profit. Profit is needed to make up for shortfalls in sales, and a great many other costs to the business. It is not a cash cow for the owner. Profit is a lifeline that gives the business an opportunity to survive into the future.

Sole proprietorships allow the owner to just dip into profits at any time because the owner and business are one entity. Partners may each spend the business's profits freely because they and the business are one entity. Incorporating a business not only protects its profits from inadvertent personal spending, it actually gives the business protection of law from owner spending because by law they are separate entities. Any money the corporation spends has to at least look like it was spent to the benefit of the corporation.

Instead of having a bunch of complex laws to set up a variety of corporations, let's just have one and keep it simple. The same simple corporation should incorporate sole proprietorships and partnerships. In fact, you wouldn't even need to call it a corporation because if there is just one kind of business, it would be simply a "business."

Most of the corporate laws on the books are there to establish tax situations. The corporate laws plus the tax laws create a system only a well-trained lawyer can figure out. We need to make them both very simple. The tax code could be written in less than five pages, and business law just needs to establish that the business and the owner are separate entities. If the owner works for the business, then he or she should get a salary that is figured into the fixed cost of the business. If the owner doesn't work for the business, then the owner shouldn't expect anything. If the owner wants his or her money back out of the company, that person just needs to find someone willing to buy his or her share of the business.

Once a business is well established, has all of its assets paid for, and has saved enough money to stay in business indefinitely, then the owner or owners may decide to declare a dividend. By law one half of a declared dividend should go to the workers and should be divided equally among the workers; position in the company and pay scale should be irrelevant. The other half of the dividend goes to the business owner or owners. The owner's half of the dividend is distributed by percent of ownership. The sole business owner who works for his company gets a full half of a dividend plus a worker's cut once a dividend is declared. Dividends need to be further broken down to ensure employees who left the company before the dividend was declared get their share in order to preclude the use of dividends as weapons. Owners, of course, need the same protection. Therefore, time with the company since the last declared dividend should figure into the computations to compute dividend distribution.

CHAPTER 41

REPLACING THE MEDICAL INDUSTRY WITH MEDICAL CARE

In order to get away from a medical system that preys on the sick and injured for profit, America needs a doctor run, government financed health care system where the labor needed to operate the system pays for itself by calculating and quantifying the labor's value and then depositing that value, in dollars, into the federal service labor account. This will free the patient of all financial cost associated with getting sick or injured. After all, people don't generally get sick or injured so that they can have medical treatment, and making medical care free is highly unlikely to change this fact.

To make the transition without an intervening loss of available medical treatment, new government operated medical facilities should be built using government labor. The labor of the design team as well as the labor of the craftsmen building the facilities will be free of taxpayer dollars because the value of their labor will be calculated, quantified, and deposited, in dollars, into the federal service labor account.

The new hospitals and clinics, staffed by workers that are not a burden to the taxpayer, can at first take Medicare and welfare patients to eliminate those costs to the taxpayer. As capacity permits, free medical care can be offered to anyone who walks through the doors. As the medical industry, through the new competition, starts losing its ability to function, the facilities and equipment it owns can be sold to the government. The staff members of the purchased facilities can seek employment in the government system, where their labor will pay for itself. Most medical workers can retain their former position with comparable pay.

The new hospitals will increase patient capacity. Patients will not need to be forced out of the hospital before they have fully recovered in order to make room for new patients. The present medical industry is geared toward maximizing profits, which means the medical industry wants all their beds to be full all the time. To accomplish this, there needs to be more sick and injured than available beds. In times of increased sickness, as during flu season, beds filled with patients end up lining the halls. Mass disasters bring about similar circumstances. This is good for the medical industry's bottom line but very bad for nurses, doctors, and especially patients.

New medical clinics will increase the overall outpatient capacity, reducing wait times to see a physician. Clinics with manpower that pays for itself and has no profit motive can operate twenty-four hours a day seven days a week. People can seek medical care as the need arises instead of waiting for open hours or overwhelming emergency room staffs, which interrupts their availability for true medical emergencies. The added capacity will also be needed for the sick and injured who now avoid seeking needed medical treatment because they can't afford the cost.

It will be some time before the new mental facilities start to have an effect on the bottom line of the present medical industry's mental facilities because the present facilities mostly cater to the mentally ill of rich families. Most mentally ill patients live on the streets because their illness precludes their ability to support themselves, much less pay for their needed treatment. Some of the lucky mentally ill have family to support them with food, clothing, and shelter, but treatment is financially out of reach.

Provisions for dental care can be built into the new medical clinics. A good many patients that have not seen a dentist in years, or possibly ever, will flood the system looking for free care of their painful neglected teeth. The existing medical industry dental clinics will probably be safe from losing the bulk of their patients for quite some time. The selling out of the privately owned dental clinics may come sooner than expected, however, because they are all just one pronouncement away from bankruptcy. The mercury-laden amalgam filling millions of dental patients' teeth is millions of lawsuits just waiting to happen.

The massive hold by the pharmaceutical Industry on the medical industry and our government can be broken with legislation eliminating the ability to patent drugs. There will be no need for government laboratories that research, develop, and manufacture pharmaceuticals to maintain any patents. A complete list of pharmaceutical formulas should already be on file with the government. If not, then our FDA has not even bothered to give the impression of doing its job. The elimination of drug patents will cause a downward spiral in the cost of pharmaceuticals. While the price drops, the government can be building, stocking, and staffing its own laboratories or simply buy up a sufficient number of existing labs to manufacture the required pharmaceuticals. Most drugs can be replaced with recommendations for better nutrition. As one smart fellow put it, good nutrition makes a lot of sense, but it doesn't make a lot of dollars. Without a profit motive, the need for the majority of pharmaceuticals will disappear.

Maintaining an illness creates more profits, so it is understandable that the American medical industry's focus on medical research is geared toward treatment rather than prevention or cure. Medical research done without a profit motive will be geared more toward prevention and cure because the medical system will be much cheaper to maintain if disease is prevented or, failing prevention, cured as soon as possible.

Medical insurance doesn't ensure that a person will not need medical treatment; it doesn't even guarantee to pay for needed medical treatment. It's simply a way to take money from healthy working people whose money would otherwise not be available to the medical industry.

The overall control of the government financed medical care system should be handled by the surgeon general with whatever staff he or she requires. An onsite administrator with medical training should administer each medical facility. A government agency should be created under the surgeon general to promote proper nutrition as a way of preventing disease and poor health.

CHAPTER 42

TOTAL EDUCATION

Overcrowded classrooms, underpaid teachers, testing-taking precedence over teaching, calorie-rich nutrition-poor lunches, and insufficient physical activity have all taken their toll on America's school system. Education is the single most important factor in building and maintaining a strong nation, and we have gone from a get-by education system to a poor system. Schools are regularly used as a reason to increase taxes, and the proposals for new taxes often succeed, so it seems apparent that I'm not the only one who realizes how important education is to our prosperity. Unfortunately, the tax increases to support our schools are often a ruse, and the collected money frequently ends up going to contractors who promise campaign contributions.

Educators are the source of education and, therefore, the contributing root to the increased value of the nation derived from education. To determine the increase in national value that can be used to calculate and quantify the labor provided by individual teachers, it is necessary to think for a minute of a nation without education and a nation with extraordinary education for its citizens. If you're having difficulty, there are plenty of nations that don't provide education for their citizens; compare them to where the United States was when we had a get-by education system. To say our nation was ten times more valuable than the uneducated nations is an understatement.

To pay for teacher labor, we can multiply the salary of each teacher by ten and credit the resulting figure to the federal service labor account. The teacher's pay, of course, will be withdrawn from the account, but nine times the cost of their labor will remain to pay for the labor of federal employees whose calculated and quantified coefficient is less than one.

Using the federal service labor account, we can double the pay of every teacher in America. This will be a good start toward improving teacher attitude as well as job satisfaction. It will be a good incentive for teachers who have left the profession for better pay to return. The pay increase will also entice more college students toward the profession.

The present number of available classrooms will necessitate the continued overcrowding for a time. New schools will need to be built to increase available classrooms to the point where there are no more than fifteen students per classroom. That number should be reduced where difficult subject matter or student ability dictates fewer students per teacher. If the number of available teachers grows faster than available classrooms, multiple teachers can be assigned to the overcrowded classrooms.

The labor needed to build new schools can be paid for from the federal service labor account, and considering the finished value of the school buildings, it shouldn't be too hard to see that craftsman labor will place more value into the federal service labor account than their wages will withdraw—more money available for the needed jobs whose coefficient is less than one. The reduction and possible elimination of labor and salary burden on the federal government should leave more than enough funds to purchase the materials needed to build and furnish our schools. The elimination of the need to pay for building, maintaining, staffing, and furnishing schools should leave plenty of funds in local governments to pay for the land on which the schools will be built.

Our present school year dates back to the days where most of America was rural, and the majority of America's citizens were farmers. Family labor was needed to plant, tend, and harvest crops. This, of course, is no longer the case. In most families both parents work outside the home in order to finance the cost of maintaining a household. The education needed to get by as a farmer was much less than is required to function in today's cybernetic world. Teachers are overwhelmed with the task of teaching everything required in the time they have available. Students that used to work hard and play harder spend sedentary time with their electronics. Kids that used to run home from school to waiting parents who had a snack ready to eat before the chores were begun now ride a bus to the vicinity of their empty house, walk the rest of the way home, and sit around unsupervised. Through the summer, schools are empty, and children sit around the house bored, wondering what to do.

It's time to extend school hours to meet and possibly exceed work hours. Three wholesome, nutritious, healthy calorie-level meals should be offered, the first of which should be before school hours begin and the last of which should be after school hours are completed. Breakfast and/or dinner can be taken with parents, but if no such meal is available at home, it can be had by early arrival at school or delayed departure. The increased number of schools should place all schools within walking distance of home. The summer, no longer needed for farm work, is very much needed to ensure our young citizens are educationally prepared to live successfully in our high-tech world. The increased school day, as well as the year-round school year, can provide time for all the instruction needed and leave time available for recreation both organized and free play.

Exercise is one of the casualties of our electronics enriched world. A full day of school will provide the opportunity to ensure children participate in physical activity such as organized sports. The reduced class sizes will make it easy to form class teams that can compete against one another. A rotating schedule can keep the recreation facilities occupied all day long by class against class competitions that span an entire class session.

All boy and all girl classes will not only facilitate the physical activity plan but also eliminate the distractions of boy/girl interactions during class. The separation of sexes will also facilitate tailoring subject matter to be of more interest to each sex. There will be plenty of time outside of class for boys and girls to interact to their hearts' content.

Students graduating from high school often find it difficult to move into the job world. They have no formal job training and in most cases have no idea what field they would find interesting. The students that continue on to college rarely know for sure what degree to pursue. Many college students give up before graduating, and even those who carry all the way through to graduation still leave college with no job experience. So whether our young adults graduate high school, drop out of college, graduate from college, or, the worst of all, drop out of high school, they enter an unforgiving world with no work ethic or job experience. It should be obvious the education process has not been completed.

Every high school student should take a series of tests that help identify the student's interest in a field of work. These tests are not foolproof and in no way should be accepted as conclusive. The information should be used as a starting point for a counselor to discuss with the student job opportunities available in the working world that the student may find interesting. The counseling sessions should not be hurried, and they should be numerous. Students before entering their senior year of high school should know for sure what career path they intend to follow. During their senior year the students can further discuss their options as necessary.

At the age of nineteen, all Americans should continue their education with job training in the career of their choosing. Once the training is completed, they should be put to work in the job of their choosing until they reach the age of twenty-two. At that time, they should be free to continue working in their job, leave their job, and seek employment with another employer, or attend college to continue on their chosen career path.

To facilitate this inclusion in our educational system, the federal government should form "the service" a nonmilitary organization similar in structure to our military. The term of active service should begin on the nineteenth birthday and end on the twenty-second birthday. The service will begin with basic training, where uniforms will be issued and indoctrination to the service will be given. After basic, the newly indoctrinated service member, wearing a service uniform that will be the sole attire until his or her twenty-second birthday, will attend a training school where he or she will learn the chosen job. After completing their training school, the service member will be put to work. Service pay will begin on the first day of service (nineteenth birthday) and continue until the conclusion of the service commitment (twenty-second birthday).

Service pay will be paid from the federal service labor account. The rate of pay will be based on time in service and will be the same for all service members regardless of job chosen.

High school dropouts should be indoctrinated into the service on the day after they drop out of high school. They should be given a job to do but not embark on their chosen career path until their nineteenth birthday. High school continuation classes can be given in the evenings after the day's work is completed. The classes should continue until graduation is achieved. The people who didn't graduate before their nineteenth birthday, for whatever reason, should also be in attendance in the high school continuation classes.

The people who decide on a career that requires college will learn a job in the service that embarks them along their chosen career path by giving them an understanding of the career field. For example a doctor may be trained as an orderly and then work in a hospital; an electrical engineer may be trained and work as an electrician; a lawyer may be trained as a legal secretary. The professional careers will each have different jobs available to choose from, any of which will provide an understanding helpful in the chosen career and will in addition give the student a job to fall back on if the final goal is not achieved.

Service members who want to get a head start in college can attend free college courses during their off-duty time. Once the service member is released from active duty, he or she will have the opportunity to continue working at the job. The former service members can take off their uniforms, and their pay will increase to the pay commensurate with their job and position. If their career choice required college, or if they just decided to go to college after working in the service, they can leave the service and go to college.

The last step in a new, exceptional education system will be college that is free of financial obligation. However, there needs to be an academic obligation. Every student should make a minimum grade in order to continue on in college.

CHAPTER 43

DAY CARE

Supporting a family on a living wage isn't enough if the family only has one adult. The adult needs a safe place where he or she can leave his or her children any time of day for as long as needed, usually no less than forty hours a week. This place also needs to be free.

We need government-run child development centers and youth centers, where parents can bring their child or children to be responsibly and safely cared for without cost. These centers should be open twenty-four hours a day seven days a week so that they are available to provide a safe place for children no matter what the work schedule or circumstance of the parents.

Granted this leaves the door open to abusing the system, but it is far better that the system be abused than the children. At times when parents reach the end of their tolerance, there will be a safe place where the child may be taken and left until sanity returns. Of course, there will be other situations equally important where it will be in the child's best interest to have a safe place to temporarily reside.

I spent a great deal of time contemplating how to deal with married service members and service members with children, whether married or not. The problem constantly arose that any extra compensation or accommodation encourages people to get married or have children.

To avoid this situation without punishing a young woman who has a child, whether by choice or by accident, I came up with the idea to have apartments available in the upper floors of service-run child development centers. A young woman who has a child before the age of nineteen will start her service in one of the centers. She will be assigned an apartment for herself and her child or children. She will receive her indoctrination while her child is safely cared for. After indoctrination, she will begin her training. If she wishes to work in the center, she will attend classes to learn to be a care provider or to accomplish some other task within the center. She will also be free to learn a job that will take her outside the center.

A girl who becomes pregnant while in the service will move into one of the apartments in the center. Nothing else needs to change. She will still accomplish the job she was trained for, and if possible at the locations where she was previously working.

Married couples will be treated the same as unmarried service members. They will each have their own apartment once their training is complete, and they are assigned to a job. If possible, they will be in the same dormitory. As with all service members, married or not, their sleeping arrangements, since they will be above the age of consent, will be their own business.

The service girls and boys that chose a career in child development will provide some of the manpower needed to care for the children in the child development center, which will be available to the general public as well as the girls living in the floors above.

CHAPTER 44

RECYCLING

Recycle centers take many discarded items and make a profit by turning them into useable products. However, there are still tons of items placed into landfills. Some of these items could be recycled profitably if they had been placed into the proper recycle container rather than the garbage can. The key word here is profit.

Where profit cannot be found, waste is what happens. Not a single item placed in the garbage cannot be recycled. Creating landfills is both a waste of land and a waste of material. The service, without concern for profit, can expend the manpower needed to extract value from our garbage.

The manpower needed for recycling everything will be far greater than the likely number of young adults who might choose a career in recycling. The solution is to make recycling a pathway to other jobs. Everyone will probably agree that working with garbage is a dirty job, and most people will also realize it can be hazardous to your health. The people who work at the recycle centers will often need to be protected from the environment in which they work. To use protective clothing takes some training. Cleaning up garbage and making it safe as well as useful is not much different than cleaning up an accidental spill of hazardous materials.

The young adults that choose to go into recycling will be trained on all the facets of recycling. In addition, they will be trained to work in hazardous materials suits and use all of the equipment needed to clean up a hazardous materials spill. In an emergency, service kids will be among the responders that take over from the emergency services personnel who stop the spill.

> *Processing resources out of our waste stream will make resources available to enter the production stream.*

CHAPTER 45

IMMIGRATION

We need a better pathway through which immigrants may gain US citizenship. The process needs to be available without delay to all who ask for it. There should be no opportunity for workers to temporarily enter the United States to work. Presently we send citizens of other countries out into mainstream America who don't speak English and who have no idea of the common cost of anything. They keep Americans from working by accepting jobs at starvation wages. They pay little or no taxes and create a drain on the social services, which are paid for with collected taxes.

I have previously suggested a service in which all nineteen- to twenty-two-year-old Americans may continue their education process to include job training and experience. Now I am suggesting that entry into the service be required for citizens of foreign countries upon being accepted for immigration to the United States. This will immediately provide them with a job without displacing an American worker. While in the service, immigrants and their families will be assigned to housing that is close to their work. They will attend classes to learn to speak English and gain an understanding of our laws and government. Other classes will be made available for the immigrants to choose from, as they like. At the end of three years of service, the immigrant will take a test for citizenship that tests his or her ability to read, write, and speak English, as well as test their understanding of our laws and government. Those who don't pass the test will be allowed to stay in the service until they can pass the test.

Under no circumstances will they be released into mainstream America without having the ability to read, write, and speak English or without an understanding of our laws and government.

During their three years of service to the United States, the FBI can run a thorough background check to determine if we have allowed a potential terrorist or habitual criminal into our country.

Presently we have millions of citizens of foreign countries living and working in the United States. Many of them are here illegally; some have overstayed their legally authorized entry to the United States for work, and others entered the United States illegally to begin with. We can establish and streamline a pathway through which immigrants may gain citizenship. Allow enough time for everyone concerned to apply and enter the service, and then start collecting those who don't take advantage of the process and are here illegally. The illegals we can take out into the desert, set them up in a camp, and let them build their detention center, where they will remain for five years. At the end of five years, we can again offer them citizenship, send them back to their country of origin, or keep them incarcerated. Those that have done nothing wrong beyond neglecting to ask to be here and enter the service will again be given the opportunity to spend three years in the service in order to gain citizenship. Those who have been determined to be undesirable for citizenship but have committed no crimes in America can be deported. Those who are criminals or terrorists can remain incarcerated.

CHAPTER 46

FEDERAL AGENCIES

The regulatory agencies of the federal government have come into existence for the protection of the citizens of the United States. However, the lobbyists of the industries from which we need protection have managed to eliminate the effectiveness of each of the protective agencies by encouraging our elected officials to enact legislation favorable to the industry but detrimental to the public, reduce the funding of these agencies, and cut their manpower.

Once we have representatives that truly represent the people, the representatives of the people need to enact laws against the conflicts of interest that allow heads of industry to step into leadership jobs of government organizations that are supposed to be watchdogs of that industry. Our representatives need to have their lawyers comb through the laws that govern our protective agencies and make sure the laws as well as the agencies are a benefit to the majority of the population. Most importantly, our representatives need to assure the agencies that are tasked with protecting us have adequate manpower and resources available to do the job assigned to them.

The Environmental Protection Agency (EPA) uses fines to enforce its rules. This results in companies figuring out if it's cheaper to pay the fines or fix the problem. Two of the results of this practice are polluted air to breath and unsafe water to drink. Lobbyists argue that an immediate shutdown of a polluter would eliminate the product the polluter provides. Point well taken, but maybe we need to do without their product while they fix the problem. A little more forethought in the start-up process of the business may create a process that doesn't pollute in the first place. The shutdown may also open up an opportunity for a competitor that doesn't pollute to enter the business. The present concern of industry, of course, is with profits. After all, "The purpose of a business is to make a profit," and those profits are needed for campaign contributions and lobbying. Real enforcement of our environmental laws might create a mind-set in industry that looks toward solutions to pollution rather than circumventing the laws or lobbying to eliminate the laws in favor of profits. The lobbying also creates special laws for an industry that allow the "special" industry to pollute because there doesn't seem to be any way around it. Power production using coal is one such industry. Proper enforcement of the laws could result in the elimination of every coal-fired power production plant in the nation. Then again, it may result in finding out that the process of cleaning the exhaust results in a nuclear fusion reaction that produces far more power than the quantity of power produced by burning the coal and letting the exhaust escape into the air. Who knows what advancements we are failing to realize because our profit makers want to continue business as usual to make their profits no matter the cost to the rest of us?

The Food and Drug Administration (FDA) has allowed a host of practices to develop that are detrimental to the health of the American public. Examples include feedlots, meat factories, chickens raised wing to wing in temperature-controlled barns, permanently caged egg laying chickens, pharmaceutical companies that test their own creations, and food with obvious contamination being allowed to stay in the food stream, to name a few. The agency needs a major increase in trained personnel. It needs laboratories where testing of all types can be accomplished. It needs legislation that gives its personnel the authority to do the job. It especially needs an upper echelon of management that is dedicated to protecting the American people and is less concerned with the profits of industry.

The FDA is supposed to be protecting us, yet food is the leading cause of death in America. The deaths that occur immediately following consumption are the result of the failings of FDA inspectors or rather the lack of inspectors. However, the majority of deaths caused by food take a shortened lifetime to occur. The food-induced deaths are slow and painful in coming. The growth of the fast-food or, if you will, inedible consumables industry is directly and indirectly responsible for many of these long-term food-induced deaths, yet the FDA has done nothing to alert the public to the dangers, much less mitigate the dangers the nutrition-deficient consumables pose. The meat factories, a direct result of the inedible consumables industry, are a blatant failing of the FDA. The first of these to appear should have been shut down immediately by the FDA. Instead we are warned that E. coli is a natural danger of meat, so the meat must be cooked long enough and at sufficient temperature to kill the E. coli. In fact, E. coli is not natural at all. It comes to us as a result of the feedlots, another failing of the FDA. Salmonella is introduced into our food supply by contaminated eggs and chickens. The FDA should have the right and responsibility to shut these types of operations down long before they become the norm.

Many people don't live long enough to die from poor nutrition and the pollutants in our food supply because they die from adverse reactions caused by legally administered prescription drugs. The FDA needs to build laboratories and employ the personnel needed to test new drugs rather than allow the pharmaceutical company that produces the drug to do its own testing.

The Securities and Exchange Commission (SEC) created after and as a result of the Great Depression of 1929 was powerless to prevent the economic disaster of 2008, partially because of its lobbying-induced reduction in manpower but mostly because lobbyists were successful in preventing the legislation of derivatives. The agency greatly needs the return of its manpower in order to protect our economy. It also needs top personnel that have the best interest of the people at heart instead of the best interest of money-breeding enterprise.

CHAPTER 47

INCOME TAX

The economists that try to lead us to believe that money trickling down through the economy creates jobs either don't understand how an economy works or purposefully mislead in order to justify tax breaks for the rich. Consumer spending is what creates jobs. Another concept many economists either don't understand or choose to remain silent about is that adequately taxing big business is necessary to maintain a strong, balanced economy while sustaining an efficient government.

Consumer spending is a brick in the foundation of a nation's economy. Personal income tax should not chip away at these bricks. Small business owners and workers alike should be left with enough income to pay for all the owners' and workers' living expenses with at least a little more for personal gratification and savings. Every adult, based on today's cost of living, should receive a $50,000 exemption on his or her federal and state income tax; children should be granted a $10,000 exemption. This means an adult couple with two children would not pay any income tax if their combined family income were less than $120,000 a year. This should be the only deduction allowed and there should be no tax credits.

The way we figure business income for the purpose of taxation should be changed significantly. First of all, the deduction from gross business income for income paid to an individual employee should be capped at $1 million. That is to say, a company can pay an employee any amount of money it sees fit, but when that business figures its taxable income, it can only deduct a maximum of $1 million of that individual's personal income payment from the company's gross income. This should in no way allow a tax break for the company or the individual from the resulting double taxation on the portion of personal pay exceeding $1 million. If a company can afford to pay an individual more than $1 million a year, it can certainly afford to pay taxes on the balance that exceeds the $1 million. Likewise, any individual that makes more than $1 million a year in income can certainly afford to pay income taxes on the entire income minus, of course, the personal deduction allowed for him or her and his or her family.

The taxable income of manufacturing businesses should equal gross income minus the cost of American-made raw materials and American labor used to manufacture the product. The country should not share the cost of purchasing a factory or the machinery within. After all, the country does not get to share ownership of the factory or its contents. Tax-deductible operating costs should certainly not include buying out a competitor. Advertising, while important to any business, should be paid out of post tax dollars. Foreign-supplied raw materials or finished goods should not be deductible from income because they produce no tax dollars for the nation.

The price of American-supplied materials includes taxes paid to the various levels of government such as income tax on American labor and sales tax on equipment needed in the processing and transportation of the materials. The cost also includes the support of one or more American businesses along with their workers. All these costs of buying American-made materials give benefit to America and its people. Buying foreign-supplied materials includes no domestic benefit to the government or American business. The only benefit derived is increased profit for the manufacturer. Refusing the subtraction of foreign-supplied materials from gross income in the computation of taxable income is fair if not equitable compensation.

The cost of American labor and American made products for resale should be the only expenses deducted from the gross income of a service-oriented business when figuring the net income on which it pays taxes. The cost of buying and maintaining the assets a service-oriented business needs to carry on its business should not be tax deductible. The country's citizens share no ownership of these items; therefore, they should share no cost in the form of reduced taxes. The costs of a company's assets are reflected in the price it charges its customers when it provides the service for which it demands payment.

Mercantile businesses should, in addition to American labor, only deduct the price of wholly American-made merchandise from their gross income for income tax purposes. The cost of doing business, including the cost of all merchandise foreign and domestic, is passed on to the customer.

It can be argued, indeed it is now the case, that all the costs of doing business should be deducted from gross income in order to arrive at net taxable income. However, where do you draw the line? Presently almost any purchase a company chooses to make, including the cost of a private jet, can and usually is considered a deduction from gross income for the purpose of deriving net taxable income. The result is many multi-billion dollar corporations end the year with no taxable income. Granted they pay their top management millions of dollars in income, fly them around the world in private jets, and give them vacations at private company-owned mansions on company estates, but they have no taxable income to show for it.

If the only deductions from gross income are those that benefit the country, such as American labor, which is already subject to income tax, and American raw materials and products, which also pay their share of taxes, then the company can charge accordingly for its products or services as it pays its full fair share of taxes.

All income tax should be figured on graduating increments of income as illustrated below. The suggested figures are a suggested starting point. Once the national debt is paid off, slight downward annual adjustments to these figures may be made to bring the monetary needs of government in line with the collected taxes. The calculations should be made to retain a surplus in the national coffers at the end of each fiscal year. Our country, like any conscientious family or business should have savings to be prepared for unexpected expenses.

Deductions from taxable income should be taken from the bottom of the income, not off the top.

Income Bracket			Suggested income tax: Federal	State	Combined
0–200,000	-	-	5%	2%	7%
200,000–400,000	-	-	10%	3%	13%
400,000–600,000	-	-	15%	4%	19%
600,000–800,000	-	-	20%	5%	25%
800,000–1,000,000	-	-	25%	6%	31%
1,000,000–1,000,000,000	-	-	33%	7%	40%
Over 1,000,000,000	-	-	40%	10%	50%

Example: a banker who is paid a salary of $10,000 a week and has a wife and two children would pay $ 54,400 income tax.

Computations: the first $200,000 of his income is taxed at 7 percent, but he has a $120,000 exemption so $80,000 times 7 percent is $5,600. The second $200,000 is taxed at 13 percent, and 13 percent of $200,000 is $26,000. The remaining $120, 000 of his annual salary is taxed at 19 percent. Nineteen percent of $120,000 is $22,800. So $5,600 plus $26,000 plus $22,800 is $54,400.

This means the banker would be left with $465,600 for the year to support his wife and two children.

Another example: a couple that earns $90,000 a year and has two children would be left with $90,000 to support their family.

Last example: a service business has a gross income of $342,982,323,544. Its labor costs are $124,836,043,026 but the salaries of three of the company's top executives exceed $1,000,000. The total pay for these three executives is $17,000,000, so $14,000,000 of the company's labor cost is not deductible. This leaves the company with a $124,822,043,026 tax deduction and, of course, the business is not a living entity, so it gets no personal exemptions.

Computations: The business's deductions exceed $1,000,000,000, so it has passed up all of the lower tax brackets and their entire taxable income is taxed at 50%. $218,160,280,518 of taxable income times 50 percent leaves a tax liability of $109,080,140,259.

This means the business will be left with $233,902,183,285 after taxes.

The federal government should collect all the income tax. In the cases where business income is generated in different states, the federal government would be tasked with figuring which part of the income was generated in each state. At the beginning of the fiscal year, all state-directed funds would be distributed to the states.

This would eliminate the need for states to make a deal to lower or eliminate taxes paid by a business in order for that business to carry on operations in the state.

The new tax code might be written on a few pages that are easily understood by all. The present volumes of tax codes, both federal and state, can be eliminated, and the armies of tax attorneys can seek more useful employment. At tax time, one simple page will be all that is needed to file income tax no matter the income level.

CHAPTER 48

TAXING DERIVATIVES

Another word for derivative is casino. If this happens, I get lots of money. If it doesn't happen, then a whole stream of money went out and nothing came in.

A 90 percent income tax on derivative income would discourage most derivative transactions. There may be those that find the transaction so important that it is worth paying 90 percent of the income gained to taxes. The 10 percent could still be millions. For the vast majority, however, we would not participate in a contract that we knew we were going to pay 90 percent of whatever income we got out of the contract to taxes, no regulatory law needed; the derivatives that now increase the price of every product we buy by an amount that goes directly to people who had nothing to do with the production of whatever it is we are buying at an increased price will no longer be raising prices.

There is an amazing array of derivatives on the market and under it. One of the more visible, if not obvious, derivatives in wide use is insurance. I'm not saying it should be spared—quite the opposite. People need to work hard, earn money, actually be paid the money, and then save for a rainy day such as the day the house burned down—thank God there was no one in it—and now we're going to have to dip into our savings a little. That is the proper response. Not, I hope the insurance covers this.

Medical insurance has proven to be detrimental to health—mental, physical, and financial. It is far better that the sick and injured and especially the mentally ill do not need to pay for treatment received. With the working class providing the manpower and those at the higher ends of the financial spectrum paying taxes, we could have a true health care system that is free to the patient.

Retirement, the second biggest recent loser to derivatives, is better served through a social security system that is a true retirement system. To fund it properly would simply require a 7 percent tax on gross income of every financial entity—in the case of humans, over the age of twenty-two. Then it doesn't matter how many people are retired and how many are working. The economy pays the retirement payments regardless of the number of workers.

Derivatives have more than tripled our gas
prices. Anyone want to keep those?

Federal Financial System

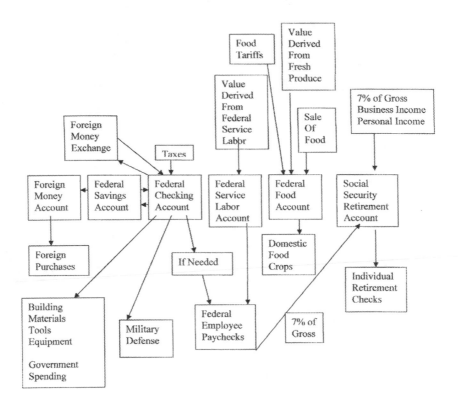

CHAPTER 49

FEDERAL FUNDING

Federal funding for the newly formed United States government came from the pockets of the rich among the conspirators who broke away from England. The system has changed a bit, but there are still strong connections between government and business finance. There is much talk about improving government by running it more like a business. The idea stems from the realization that the government is not operating with cooperation and coordination toward a specific goal; in the case of business, that would be making a profit. The government, of course, can't make a profit because it doesn't make a good to sell and should not charge for its services. Business, with its pursuit of profits, creates less than favorable working conditions for its employees and less than adequate goods and services for its customers. The government, with no clear goal, creates havoc for business and citizens alike.

New goals for business have already been suggested. The one underlying goal for government should be serving its citizens. Other objectives can spring from this one goal with the primary focus being on what is best for the country and its citizens. The government shouldn't be borrowing money from or lending money to business. Neither is in the best interest of the country or its citizens. Subsidizing business is also not in the best interest of the country or its citizens. Money flowing from government coffers into business should be through the paychecks of government workers, retirement checks of Social Security recipients, and the government purchase of products. Service is what the government does, not something it pays business to do.

Crediting money to accounts within the government based on the increased value of the country derived from labor and the growing of food places money where it is needed to compensate the workers whose labor produced the value. It even leaves money available to pay some if not all the government employees, whose work, although necessary, produces no value to the country. The benefits to the economy are twofold. There is not an unnecessary drain on the economy to pay for labor that has its own intrinsic value, and the money spent by government workers places money into the economy. Consumer spending is the foundation on which an economy rests. The contribution of money into the economy through government paychecks helps the economy operate and grow.

Crediting money to the federal food account ensures money is available to pay farmers for their labor, but more importantly, it assures a steady flow of food, something that is needed by every citizen.

The proposed federal financial system is simple and provides savings from which unexpected expenses can be funded. Complicating the system is only needed by those seeking to move federal money into private pockets.

CHAPTER 50

SOCIAL SECURITY

Under the pretence of helping the country's economy recover from the recession of 2008, the US government bailed out the big banks that created and were heavily invested in the derivatives that caused the fall. Many retirement account managers had invested the funds under their control in the same type of derivatives. The retirement funds, however, were not bailed out, and millions of Americans lost their ability to retire.

Due to many workers regularly changing their place of employment, IRAs and 401s, which depend heavily on dollars contributed and the performance of the investment, have replaced the old guaranteed retirement provided by long-term employers. IRAs and 401s have been shown time and again to be unreliable as a sole source plan for retirement.

The Social Security System, which was established as a supplemental retirement system, should be modified to create a full retirement system that can support retired workers in a manner they have become accustomed to through their working years. To this end, there should be no cap on the income on which Social Security withholding is paid. In addition, businesses should contribute to the Social Security Retirement System at the same rate as individuals. In this way, businesses will be contributing to the retirement of their employees as well as the retirements of the owners.

A cap of $20,000 monthly should be placed on income derived from Social Security. If this seems excessive, then consider: anyone who can qualify for a payment this large has paid a great deal of money into the

Social Security Retirement System. If you think $20,000 a month is not enough for those who have paid millions into the system, then realize they probably don't need Social Security anyway.

Social Security withholding should not start until after a citizen's twenty-second birthday. This still leaves plenty of time for Social Security contributions. To fully fund the Social Security Retirement System, 7 percent of gross income (personal and business) should be paid into Social Security (no cap).

Eligibility for collecting Social Security benefits should begin at age fifty-two. The total Social Security retirement payment should be figured by multiplying ½ percent times the number of quarters worked times the base figure (see chart). Example: retiring at age fifty-two with 120 quarters of income would mean Social Security retirement would be equal to 60 percent of the average of the highest eighty quarters of income on which 7 percent of income was paid to Social Security.

If a person works continuously from age twenty-two until age seventy-two (two hundred quarters) before they start collecting Social Security, their monthly payment will be 100 percent of their highest quarter income up to the $240,000 annual cap.

Only personal income on which Social Security payments were made should be used to figure benefits. This prevents the people who enjoyed the benefit of the income cap heretofore placed on Social Security income from capitalizing on funds they didn't contribute.

If a claimant continues to work after he or she begins to collect Social Security, then his or her percentage would increase annually on the anniversary of his or her claim, but the base would remain constant.

The chart shows the manner in which the base payment for Social Security is set by age. Social Security benefits are figured on quarterly income.

Age	Average if Highest Quarters of Income
52	average of highest eighty quarters of income
53	average of highest seventy-six quarters of income
54	average of highest seventy-two quarters of income

55 average of highest sixty-eight quarters of income
56 average of highest sixty-four quarters of income
57 average of highest sixty quarters of income
58 average of highest fifty-six quarters of income
59 average of highest fifty-two quarters of income
60 average of highest forty-eight quarters of income
61 average of highest forty-four quarters of income
62 average of highest forty quarters of income
63 average of highest thirty-six quarters of income
64 average of highest thirty-two quarters of income
65 average of highest twenty-eight quarters of income
66 average of highest twenty-four quarters of income
67 average of highest twenty quarters of income
68 average of highest sixteen quarters of income
69 average of highest twelve quarters of income
70 average of highest eight quarters of income
71 average of highest four quarters of income
72 highest quarter of income

Base figure is constant once you start collecting benefits.

To encourage working class participation in Congress, after the individual passes his or her fiftieth birthday, there should be special Social Security retirement benefits. For instance, his or her retirement base figure could be based solely on his or her congressional income. Social Security retirement for any congressman elected before his fiftieth birthday should be figured in the normal manner as any person who has never served in Congress.

Social Security payments should be tripled for those currently collecting Social Security. This will allow time for the refiguring of benefits and offer immediate economic relief.

CHAPTER 51

FIXING THE BANKS

Banks don't like government-imposed regulation. They feel they should be free to operate and regulate themselves. After the Great Depression a very complex set of government regulation was imposed. The banks, after many years of somewhat successful regulation, convinced our elected officials to lift the regulations. The deregulation brought us right back to the brink of financial destruction that the banks brought us to before they were initially regulated.

Despite these unfortunate occurrences, I honestly believe it is in the best interest of the economy to let the banks regulate themselves with just these few minor laws to guide their way.

Banking Rules

1. Banks cannot charge more than 3 percent interest, but they may charge less.
2. The total money a bank may loan can add up to no more than 20 percent of the money its depositors have placed in savings accounts.
3. The bank is responsible for all nonpayment of loans. No loss may be passed on to depositors.
4. The banks' operating capital and profits are earned through the collection of the interest paid for loaning the allowed portion of

depositor savings. The banks are not allowed to charge a fee for any services rendered to customers or to other banks.

5.   Nonbank entities may loan money, but they cannot collect interest on the loaned money or charge a fee for the service of loaning the money. Increasing the price of a purchased item bought with credit is considered charging a fee.

These simple laws will hardly make it worthwhile for banks to loan money to private individuals. This is as it should be. Working people should make enough money to pay for a good living for themselves and their families. Their income should include enough money for them to save regularly. Their savings should be used to acquire the things that cannot be purchased with the remains of one paycheck. Savings should also be available for the occasional unexpected expense. Using credit to make personal purchases is never a good idea.

Because of the danger of organized crime taking advantage of these laws, there should be extended stay (ten years plus) jail sentences for *all* personnel involved with charging illegal interest or fees, *plus* massive fines for the businesses that violate these laws.

The workingman wants to take his paycheck to the bank, deposit some money in savings for big wants and rainy days, and have the rest of his check available to pay bills and make purchases. He or she wants this money to flow in and out of the bank without effort or cost to the depositor. People also want all of their money to be there when they want it; no excuses from the bank are acceptable.

The entrepreneur wants to go to the bank for extra capital when needed to make a larger profit or stay in business. A business is in the position to use borrowed money to increase its profits and let the increase pay the cost of repaying the loan's principle with interest.

The consumer benefits when a business uses a bank loan to create an increase in available goods and services. The consumer also benefits when a business in need of quick cash to stay in business gets the loan needed to continue providing a good or service to the consumer.

The banker, who throughout history has always managed to scramble to the top of the financial food chain, is nothing more than a businessman. The fact that his business is handling large quantities of money should in no way entitle him or her to a larger paycheck than similar labor would yield.

A well-run bank benefits everyone. The costs associated with running a bank can be minimal. When everyone who wants a job can have a job that pays a living wage from which a substantial percentage can be saved each month, then the depositors needed to finance the creation and operation of a bank can be found in a relatively small geographical area.

CHAPTER 52

FUNDING A BUSINESS

A business should choose one of four ways to acquire the funding needed to come into existence. One is for the new business owner to have all the funds needed in savings. Another is for several individuals to get together and each contribute an amount of money from his or her savings. Borrowing money from a bank is also an option. The last of the four options is to sell stock in the new business to strangers. All four options suggested can originate from the savings accounts of individual workers. The first and second options are directly from individual savings. The third, a bank loan, is taken from the personal savings of others as the bank loans out money in order to collect interest income, which is needed to cover the costs of running the bank. Stocks, the last option, should only be purchased with savings that are excess and can be lost without financial injury.

Banks provide storage and movement of money as a service to the depositors. It is a benefit to both the depositors and the bank to loan out a small amount of the stored money at interest. The banker can cover all of the operating expenses of the bank with the collected interest, and the depositor can have his or her money safely stored and instantly and safely transported to the location of his or her choice without charge. The business must prove to the bank that a sound, presently underfunded business opportunity is at hand and that the profits made will be sufficient to ensure the survival of the business and pay back the loan with interest.

Stocks are a way for people to invest in a business they think is worthy of their support. It is in the best interest of everyone to allow the new owner or potential owner to know as much as possible about the business, especially its financial situation. If the business is not as valuable as it was when the owner, who now wants to sell, bought it, then the owner lost money. The owner shouldn't try to pass on the loss to an unsuspecting newcomer. The stockholder was in ownership of the business as the business lost money. A loss that can't be hidden gives more incentive toward preventing the loss.

Funding business doesn't need to be complicated. Making it complicated creates ways to skim money out of the economy without placing a good or service of equal value into the economy.

CHAPTER 53

REINDUSTRIALIZING OUR NATION

In the proposed system of economics and politics, everyone who wants a job can have a job that pays, at a minimum, a living wage, which includes money left over for wants and savings. Consumers with money to spend need products to buy, and this creates business opportunity for those who want to create those products. The multi-corporate conglomerates, which have used economy of scale together with inequitable tax codes to destroy small privately owned business, don't care about the product they offer to the consumer. They care about increasing their profits. The proof rests on every shelf of every store in America.

The revised tax codes, together with the poor-quality merchandise offered by the big conglomerates, offer an opportunity for small business to make a comeback. The pathway begins with designing the best product a prospective business owner can develop. These brave new business owners must make their products out of the best material, use the greatest care in their manufacturing processes, and ensure they present a product built to last to fully compete against the massive conglomerates, as well as each other.

The elimination of patents might go a long way toward making superior products available to the consumer, such as cars that can travel

80 miles on a gallon of gasoline and are big enough for a tall person to sit in comfortably.

Service is another place the big conglomerates open a door for competition. The conglomerates don't care about their employees, and in turn the employees don't care about their employers or the customers that keep their employers in business. A small business owner has the opportunity to know each employee personally. The care shown by an employer toward his or her employees is carried forward to the customer.

Customers who get good service and quality products are going to come back, and they will recommend the business to their friends, relatives, and acquaintances.

A business doesn't have to be very big to support a family. The customer base of a small town can support a seamstress who really cares about the quality and fit of the clothes he or she produces. A small building, a modest amount of equipment, and several seamstress customers can provide the basis of a business for a manufacturer of high quality cloth. The equipment used by the cloth manufacturer is specialized. An engineer that understands the process of making cloth can build a business by designing the equipment needed to make quality cloth and then furnish a machine shop to make the equipment. The business owner, the few machinists needed to operate the machines, and a few supplemental employees can all make a comfortable living providing needed machinery to start-up cloth manufactures. The textile industry is just a minor example. There are a plethora of potential products that could be manufactured by new small businesses.

The smaller a business stays, the lower its tax rate. The massive conglomerates will likely be in the highest tax brackets, and without their tax write-offs of old a large portion of their massive income will go toward paying off the national debt and supporting government operation. The massive conglomerates will be forced to charge a much higher price for their inferior products. The economy of scale that destroyed the small businesses will be tipped in favor of small business. Caring service and quality products will further tip the scales, and small business can make a comeback.

The massive manufacturing conglomerates are internationally owned companies and have mostly moved their manufacturing overseas. Disallowing the deduction from income of all foreign-made goods and foreign-supplied raw materials will in effect bring back the tariffs, which corporate America lobbied to eliminate. This will place domestic manufacturers back on a more equal footing with foreign manufacturers. Conglomerate retailers, with their massive income and therefore massive taxes, will also lose ground to small retailers, which will reverse the process that a few decades ago destroyed the small manufactures that used to provide quality products to the small retailers.

CHAPTER 54

SETTING THE STAGE

It will all begin when the majority in each congressional district figure a way to select a person from among them that has labored at a common job his or her whole life and understands what it is like to live paycheck to paycheck and be regularly forced to accept credit for the items that are purposefully priced above the price level that a working person can afford to pay with saved money. To fully understand the working class, which accounts for the majority of Americans, a person must live the life of a common laborer. Using the "write-in" box to circumvent the money-intensive electoral system the rich minority has built can fill the House of Representatives with people who truly understand how the majority of America lives.

A Congress friendly to the majority would make laws that are good for the majority and eliminate some of the laws that are only good for a few and very bad for the majority.

Income tax laws, for instance, could be written in about five pages, at least one of which could repeal all the volumes of tax laws that now make it possible for the richest individuals and businesses to pay little or no taxes. A simple graduating income tax with few exemptions or deductions would be most fair for the majority. Businesses will find it easier to include their income tax in the price of their product if they start their tax year with a good idea of what their tax liability for the year will be. A graduating tax will also make it possible for small businesses to compete with large businesses.

A Congress friendly to the majority would create a Social Security system that actually allows a working class individual to retire. The majority are in great need of a true retirement system that they can count on for a secure retirement instead of gambling on an overinflated stock market and financial system to give an adequate income that will last until the last breath is drawn. The reality is the stock market and bogus retirement investments will eventually leave millions of people without an income at a time when they can't gainfully employ themselves. A 7 percent tax on the gross income of every entity, human and business alike, should be sufficient to fund the system indefinitely.

A Congress friendly to the majority would recognize that labor has value and declare that the increased value of the country created by government labor to be a basis for backing the money used to pay government workers. Once all the legislation and calculations are completed and the federal government establishes the "federal service labor account" it will be possible to place every teacher, police officer, and firefighter in the country on the federal payroll. This will free up local tax dollars, which were paying wages, to be used to pay for the equipment and supplies needed for these public servants to do their jobs.

Without the need to consider meager wages of local citizens to draw on for support of schools and staff, teachers' pay can finally be raised to a level commensurate with their education and training. The draw back into the teaching profession, which many left for lack of proper pay, will leave many open jobs in the wake. Reducing the number of students per teacher will increase the demand for teachers. A small class size will necessitate more schools to house the extra classrooms that will be needed.

School buildings can also be built with government labor, paid from the "federal service labor account"; of course, the craftsmen's labor will place more value into the federal service labor account than it will take away because each school built will increase the value of the United States by much more than the cost of the combined wages paid for labor and the cost of the materials to build the school.

A Congress friendly to the majority would increase the staff of police departments to 100 percent, thus enabling them to do their job instead of just documenting the wrong inflicted daily on our citizens; of course, eliminating the revolving doors on our legal system will help a great deal more, but that is another book.

Firefighters are wonderful; you call them, and they come, and when they come they bring hundreds of thousands of dollars worth of equipment with them that they will use to help the caller in any way they can. At the conclusion of their service, they say, "Hope the rest of your day goes better," and depart without any question of payment ever being raised. However, if you let them transport you to a hospital for any reason, the first question out of a hospital attendee's mouth will be, "How is the patient going to pay?"

A Congress friendly to the majority would build hospitals and staff them with manpower that pays for itself, thus opening the door to a medical care system that doesn't need to charge its patients or limit its services available.

A Congress friendly to the majority would build a health care system that has enough excess capacity to handle mass disasters and severe outbreaks of infection. The whole emergency services system needs to be expanded to handle any type of emergency imaginable. The only way this can be done is to realize that the labor expended to make the system work has value that can be used to pay employee wages.

Money available to pay government workers without a corresponding tax drain on the economy will make it possible to pay every government worker a wage sufficient to pay for transportation, a place to live, food to eat, clothes to wear, and more. Doubling the number of teachers, adequately manning emergency services, bringing the personnel of the medical community into the civil service, building a plethora of federal buildings may collectively eliminate unemployment. However, chances are it won't because all of the above jobs require knowledge and job skill to perform, and our children leave school with no job skills.

A Congress friendly to the majority would extend the years of education to include training so that every individual will be able to learn a job of each individual's choosing and to allow the individual to gain work experience at the given job for pay. The period of job training should span the time between each individual's nineteenth and twenty-second birthday. The pay doesn't need to be much because while our children are in the job training and the working phase of their education, they should live free of charge in a single apartment, wear nothing but issued uniforms, have free food available at a dining hall within their apartment building, and have free transportation available to get to their job. With as much help as needed, half their pay should be invested in the stock market. One forth of their pay should be placed in savings and the other fourth should be enough to pay for their incidentals and any food items they wish to prepare for themselves. By the time they reach their twenty-second birthday, they should not only have a job skill and a good work ethic but have an understanding of investing; they will have money invested, and they will have a savings account. At the age of twenty-two their education should, at their choosing and demonstrated ability, continue, free of charge, to whatever education level they desire and can achieve.

The process of training our youth to become a responsible workforce is the subject of *The Service*, a book that graphically illustrates the process and then goes on to show what a truly democratic service-oriented government would look like. The book also talks about how we can fairly deal with our immigrants. The present system, or rather lack of, is the result of the desires of the rich minority to have ultra-cheap labor at their disposal. Immigrants need to have a place to live, food to eat, and clothes to wear, just like every other individual. In addition, most also need to learn to read, write, and speak English in order to function in America. They also need to understand their rights and responsibilities under the law.

A Congress friendly to the majority would offer citizenship in exchange for three years of service, during which a place to live, food to eat, and clothes to wear were provided. Then we would have the opportunity to give job training, if needed, and provide jobs that are a benefit to the country. Isolating the immigrants during their term of service will help with the communication difficulties as well as provide an opportunity to get to know each individual we allow into our country before they are allowed free run of the country.

There are thousands of square miles of unused land along our southern border. This would be a good place to build service training centers for our youth. As a training exercise, we can have military civil engineering units build tent cities on selected properties. The tent cities can provide living quarters for the units while they build eight-story dormitories with one-, two-, and three-bedroom apartments on the second through eighth floors, fully furnished if needed. The first floor of each dormitory can house a dining hall and recreation facilities. The first and second floors, below ground level, can house classrooms, and the third level below ground can be a parking garage for service vehicles.

Immigrants and their families can occupy the dormitory buildings as soon as they are completed. The immigrants, trained in construction, can build the dormitories, training buildings, recreation facilities, medical centers, and all the other buildings needed to house the service training centers. The children of the immigrants can attend school in the classrooms during the day, and the adults can use the classrooms at night to learn to read, write, and speak English, followed by instruction on our laws and government. Once these are completed, other classes may be given to fit the needs and desires of the occupants. The adults who are not trained in construction can fill the non-construction-related jobs of the community as much as possible.

The completed fully staffed and furnished facilities of the service training centers will be available for use by the immigrants and their families as well as for the nineteen- to twenty-two-year-old Americans of the service and, of course, for civil service personnel. The civil service dormitories will have the same one-, two-, and three-bedroom apartment arrangements as the foreign service dormitories, but the nineteen- to twenty-two-year old-service members' dormitories will consist of one-bedroom studio apartments, with full kitchen and bathroom facilities, so that each service member can enjoy his or her own living quarters, maybe for the first time in his or her short life.

All staff jobs can go to foreign service members as much as possible, considering current job skills of the available personnel. Personnel who need training should get it prior to starting work, and this should have no effect on their living arrangements, salary, or term of service. At the end of immigrants' foreign service commitment, they will be American citizens and can continue working at their present job, with a few changes, or leave the service facility in which they live and find gainful employment in private industry.

Instead of a token salary that would never be considered a living wage, the new American citizens that choose to stay in their present jobs will receive a wage commensurate with their job and skill level, never less than a living wage. They will need to buy their own clothes; a foreign service uniform will no longer be appropriate, and they will need to begin paying rent on the apartment they have been living in if they choose to keep it.

If we have so many immigrants that we fill all our manpower requirements needed to build and staff all our service training centers, or when the centers are all completed, we can start building a flex city somewhere that is presently totally unoccupied and as central as possible in the United States. The Nevada desert is probably the best location.

A flex city can be used when a city or region needs to be evacuated for the safety of the occupants. The design used for the foreign service dormitories could work well for all the non-service (nineteen to twenty-two) occupants of the flex city whether civil service, foreign service, or visitor. The classrooms may serve various other purposes in the flex city dormitories, such as grocery and other stores, and the parking garage should be another building dedicated to parking located on the outskirts of the city.

The hub, exact center, of the flex city will be a train station for the city's subway. Rails will extend away from the city's hub in eight directions. The last stop for four of the rail lines will be parking garages. At intervals, rails will connect the eight extending rails, forming inner underground circles around the circular city.

The buildings closest to the city's hub will be the major medical centers and office buildings. The offices should be available at the same daily rate whether the renter needs one office or multiple buildings filled with offices for a day or six years. The surface roads should be laid out similar to the tracks below them. The circular city should have buildings of varied use but similar outward design as much as possible to reduce design and building costs. As the distance between the spokes grows, there will be space to fit bigger buildings, such as sports stadiums.

With a complete subway system, surface roads can be mostly bare of traffic, making them easier and safer to cross on footpaths and bicycle roads. The level below the street can be mostly open to foot traffic between buildings similar to a massive shopping mall. Of course, the city will need to be built out of wholly noncombustible materials so that it won't burn; it will need a state of the art complete fire detection system so that the fire department will know as soon as a fire does start, a complete fire suppression system to keep the fire small, and a fully manned and outfitted fire department to prevent a conflagration when the fire gets really big.

The end of the other four rail lines, on the outskirts of the city, is where the trains from every major population center in the country will come in. Single destination trains can travel at incredible speed, and they can be powered by electricity. A person could travel from New York City to Salt Lake City, change trains, and travel to Miami faster than he or she could travel from New York City to Miami by jet. This means that a person can travel from any major population center to any other major population center in two train rides. From the major population centers, the rest of the country is not far away, and if it is, then we can have some terminals in not so populated areas.

If we haven't run out of immigrants by the time the flex city is complete, then foreign service personnel can help build the tubes the trains will run through. There are more jobs to be done in this country than all our citizens put together could accomplish. Everyone needs a safe, warm place to live, appropriate for the weather clothes to wear, and healthy food to eat in sufficient quantities to physically prosper—at least and no less. For those who are willing to work, they should get everything they need and more because, as stated, our manpower and available resources can provide everyone in America with everything they need and more.

A Congress friendly to the majority would understand that anyone who wants a job should have a job that pays no less than a living wage.

A Congress friendly to the majority would establish employment centers where everyone who wants a job can walk in and get a job in an occupation they are trained for and at a wage commensurate with their job and skill level, never less than a living wage. The employment office will also be a place where businesses can find employees. The employment office needs to assure businesses have priority over government as much as possible where manpower is concerned because business supplies the goods and services that make up the economy.

After assuring the local businesses have adequate manpower, the employment office can decide how to best use the available manpower: build a youth center or a school, or fill various government open positions. The jobs filled will also depend on the longevity of the available workers. Maybe the person who walks into the employment office is an electrician and her regular employer doesn't need her today, or for the rest of the day, or for the next two weeks, maybe a month, or two. Farmers may need gainful employment when they aren't farming.

A Congress friendly to the majority would understand that buildings erected for public use can all be found to have increased the value of the United States by a specific amount. The manpower to build them plus the materials used are the cost of the building. The value depends on many factors, but the factors can all be figured and used to calculate the increase in the value of the United States that the particular building created. Subtract the materials cost from the calculated increased value of the country, and you have the value of the manpower expended. Divide the value of the manpower by the number of man-hours worked, and you have the value of each hour worked on the project. The actual calculated value of a worker's labor is irrelevant when you are figuring his government pay. Labor is paid at the prevailing wage for the worker's line of work and skill level, never less than a living wage. If the calculated value assigned to each worker's hourly labor is divided by the actual pay the worker receives, then you will have a factor. This factor can be multiplied times the hourly wage each time a craftsman in that particular craft is paid for an hour of labor. The resulting figure in dollars will be credited to the federal service labor account from which the payment for all government labor, no matter the job's factor, will be taken.

A Congress friendly to the majority would understand that factors for government jobs unrelated to construction can also be calculated and quantified. The process for many will be different, in some cases easier and in others more difficult than figuring the factors of the construction trades. But the value of all government employment can be calculated and factors found, never less than zero.

Government labor that essentially pays for itself with its derived value will open the door to offering a job to anyone who wants a job without a corresponding tax drain on the economy. The infusion of money into the economy by the government employee members of the working class will strengthen the foundation of the economy that working class wages from every source combined provides.

A Congress friendly to the majority would understand that eliminating the need for consumer credit by ensuring that every worker receives adequate pay will take away the opportunity for using fancy finance to swindle goods and services away from those who earned them.

A Congress friendly to the majority would ensure that the public protection agencies such as the FDA, OSHA, EPA, SEC, and others are fully manned with qualified personnel and that all promotions go to those within the agency who have shown they are fully qualified to accept the responsibility. A Congress friendly to the majority would realize that it is a conflict of interest to appoint the heads of these agencies from the leaders of the industries the agencies are overseeing.

A Congress that cares about the people would really care about the children. What are we doing in this country about the children who lose their parents and have no one to turn to? I'm not going to answer that because it infuriates me to think about it. Instead, I am going to say what we should do. We should build campuses where there are dormitories for the children to live in. The dormitories could be similar to the service dormitories with the exception that across the hall from each standard studio dorm room is a room that takes up the same space but is set up with two bathrooms instead of one and two sets of bunk beds in the room between the bathrooms, a study center for each child would complete the space. The service member in the studio room would be the big brother or sister, figuratively, of course, of the four children of similar age in the room across the hall. The rooms in the floors below ground level could be used for storage. Orphans could possibly come with a lot of baggage they don't need at the moment. The dorm room arrangement described would serve well for ages one through fourteen. The bunk beds, of course, would be traded for cribs with the younger ones, and the study centers would become changing centers. For everyone fifteen years and older the standard service dormitory will be appropriate. Each child can have his or her own studio apartment and one or more of the occupants on the floor will be service members that are counselors to the orphans. The children of a family may not be sleeping in the same dormitory, but they will be on the same campus, and there will be plenty of opportunity to get together and take advantage of the amazing facilities available to everyone living on the campus. The campus will contain all the classrooms in which the children will attend their classes until their nineteenth birthday. There should be no need for the children to ever leave the campus. That's not to say they should be prisoners confined to the campus, just that all their needs should be met on the campus. Hopefully they will have family and friends to visit on the outside. But they shouldn't be tortured with the thought anymore than necessary if they don't have anyone outside the campus.

The orphan campuses should be plentiful. If they are only filled to one tenth of their capacity, that is a good thing. The kids can get a lot of extra attention. The travel to their new place of residence, until their nineteenth birthday, should be as short as possible for the child who just lost everything. He or she should still be close enough for the people that know them to see them. It is also possible there may be another part of the country that would be best because family lives nearby. An orphan's nationality should not be held against him or her. If orphan children want to immigrate to the Unites States because they know we will treat them well, then they shouldn't have any less opportunity to immigrate than an adult. The orphans can do their three-year service obligation in the regular service instead of the foreign service since they will already likely read, write, and speak English; besides, their friends will all be going into the regular service. Of course, at the age of nineteen the foreign-born orphan should have the option of skipping the service and going back to his or her country of origin. At completion of service on his or her twenty-second birthday, any foreign-born orphan should have the opportunity to become an American citizen or return home to his or her native country. After all, returning with a job skill and experience is far better than returning without it.

What about the kids that have parents but the parents aren't available right now? Should we penalize the parents for having kids or going to work? Let's see which one will enable us to get the most money out of them? The question really has nothing to do with the parents; there is a child who needs someone to take care of him or her because the child is too young to take care of himself or herself. Let's not worry about the reason, the hour, or the length of stay. Let's make sure the child has a safe place to go—someplace that is familiar and comfortable. The idea of charging the child for services rendered is ridiculous, and payment should not be sought from anyone else either.

Major day care centers can be located on the ground floor of a service dormitory. The upper floors of these particular service dormitories can be filled with fully furnished two-bedroom apartments. The service girls that have a child can occupy the two-bedroom apartments. The girls can leave their child or children on the first floor on their way to work or trade school. Of course, the girls with children who decide to become child-care professionals will already be at work or school, depending on their stage. The dining hall found in every other service dormitory, no matter the service, will not be necessary for the special dormitories housing major child development centers. The entire street level floor can be dedicated to child care. The kitchen for food preparation will be below the street level, as will all the other operations necessary but not directly linked to caring for children. Dining will be done in the care rooms. The residences on the second through eighth floors will all have full kitchens in which the mothers can make meals for their family. The fathers, if between the ages of nineteen and twenty-two, will have their own studio apartment in a standard service dormitory; eating and sleeping arrangements are up to the parties involved.

Minor day-care centers will be more prevalent and in less populated areas. The facilities will be first class because we care about our customers, the babies, even if they don't pay or even leave a tip. Service boys and girls who want to work in child development and civil service employees fully trained in child development will man all the child development centers.

Of course, children that are old enough to take care of themselves to a degree would like the freedom to do those things and have help where needed. Youth centers may be much more appropriate for children old enough to take care of their toilet needs and feed themselves as long as the food is provided. Each child should have some say in which they attend; both should be open to them.

A Congress friendly to the majority would care about the elderly. Those who don't need the help of the medical profession, in the way of a nursing home, mental institution, hospital, specialty center, or anything else the medical care system offers to help every citizen live comfortably to the oldest age possible, might like a place to go where they can do things with people their own age. Senior centers can be on the list of things the town, city, or county will build as soon as the labor becomes available. Making sure everyone who wants a job can have a job that pays no less than a living wage will provide manpower for a great many nice to have buildings, each of which will increase the value of the United States to some degree.

Of course, buildings are not the only thing available manpower can build. The roads will be maintained by service and full-time civil service employees, but as manpower becomes available, we might decide to build new roads in nice to have places. Service personnel learning road construction can practice their intended trade by building bicycle roads across the country using miniature machines that are exact duplicates of the full-size road building machines.

CHAPTER 55

CONCLUSION

When everyone who wants a job can have a job that pays a living wage, then everyone that works at least forty hours a week will have enough money to provide a warm place to live, food to eat, and clothes to wear for themselves and their dependents. Everyone that works will have a savings account; most will have a substantial balance. The workers that have worked more than twenty years could have savings account balances that provide enough money to replace the house they live in and still have enough money in their saving account to buy the house again.

When everyone who wants a job can have a job that pays a living wage, then everyone that works will have the opportunity to save the recommended double the equity in the house they own outright and much more. Enough more in-fact, that the excess savings of just a few workers could be sufficient to totally finance a manufacturing business in which they all can work.

When everyone who wants a job can have a job that pays a living wage, then every business can count on consumers having enough money to buy the business's product at the price necessary to cover all costs of producing the product plus sustain a profit that will allow the business to survive. The question then, as it always should be, is do the consumers want the product? If the answer is yes, but the market is saturated, the manufacturer can rest assured someone in the world will want the manufactured product. The manufacturer can continue making the product and ship it, find a new product to make, or close the doors on the business and go to work somewhere doing a job he or she is trained for and wants to do, at no less than a living wage.

As long as business investors never invest the money they need to survive, now or in the future, and don't commit themselves to future payments that they, instead of the business with its profits to draw from, will be obligated to make, then a business owner need make no income from the business he or she owns but doesn't work in because anyone who wants a job can have a job that pays a living wage, so the owner can work elsewhere and survive. If he or she works, instead, for his or her own company, then of course he or she, like any of the business's workers, should be assured of making the regular paycheck, which is no less than a living wage.

Business owners should never take anything from their business before the business is strong enough to survive without whatever is being taken. At the point anything is taken by the owner or owners, it should be taken as a declared dividend and split 50 percent for the owners, to be shared in proportion to percentage of ownership, and 50 percent for the workers, to be divided equally for each hour worked by all the employees who have worked for the company since the last dividend was declared.

When everyone who wants a job can have a job that pays a living wage, then there will be no reason to leave people who don't want to work, or can't work due to sickness or injury, without shelter, wholesome food to eat, clothes to wear as appropriate, and all the care they need. If they simply don't want to work and have no mental or physical conditions that preclude them taking care of themselves, then those people who want a job can build poorhouses for those people who don't want to work. The poorhouses will be of the same design as the civil service/foreign service dormitories. The apartments, of course, will be free of charge; food will be provided free for everyone in the dining room, located on the street-level floor. Those who want to cook for themselves can get fresh produce in one of the below-ground rooms. Others of the below-ground rooms will contain racks and shelves of free second-hand items as well as surplus new items for the taking or borrowing as appropriate or desired.

An economy is made up of nothing more than goods and services. Work accomplished entitles the worker to a share of goods and services, but more importantly work accomplished provides the goods and services of the economy. Modern labor-saving devices and machinery, together with adequate resources in America, including manpower, make it possible for everyone in America to have a warm place to live, wholesome food to eat, clothes to wear, and a great deal more, including as much personal care as their physical condition dictates. This means the economy can withstand the effect of everyone in the economy having enough money to buy the assets they need to survive and a great deal more. It also means those in need can have the goods and services needed to keep them alive and as healthy as possible provided, without them first needing to do any work.

A city filled with workers that all have substantial savings accounts can support a number of banks, each with enough deposited saving on account to make a sizable quantity of dollars out of just 20 percent of the savings on deposit by the depositors. The bank, loaning up to 20 percent of its savings on deposit and charging 3 percent interest on the loaned amount, could be a business that makes enough profit to survive indefinitely while ensuring 100 percent of its depositors' assets. The loaned money, up to 20 percent of savings on account, could finance many new and existing business ventures.

The special financing available through complicated transactions is not needed to fill the financial needs of the economy; it is needed to fill pockets with unearned income. The word "stealing" comes to mind. Working people with money to save can finance their own business ideas to a great extent, which is why the banks need to leave 80 percent on deposit available for the depositors' use at any given time. The banks, with their ability to loan up to 20 percent of the total combined balances of all savings on deposit in their bank, will have money available to finance the more expensive business ventures. A simple stock market can be used to finance the really big money-making ventures because millions of workers will have hundreds of thousands of dollars each at their disposal to invest if they care to invest. They may not all choose to invest, but the ventures that are really worthwhile will find the needed financing from the individuals living in a relatively small geographic area.

When everyone who wants a job can have a job that pays a living wage, then anyone who steals will be stealing because he or she wants to steal and not stealing in order to feed him- or herself, or a family.

RECOMMENDED BOOKS

Aftershock, by David Wiedemer

Too Big To Fail, by Andrew Ross Sorkin

Confidence Men, by Ron Suskin

The Trillion Dollar Meltdown, by Charles R. Morris

The Looting Of America, by Les Leopold

Bet the Farm, by Frederick Kaufman

America's Bubble Economy, by David Wiedemer

Fool's Gold, by Gillian Tett

How Markets Fail, by John Cassidy

The China Study, by T. Colin Campbell, PhD, and Thomas M. Campbell II, MD

Superfoods, by David Wolfe

RECOMMENDED DVD S

Inside Job

Fresh

King Corn

Super Size Me

Two Angry Moms

We Feed the World

The Flaw

The Men Who Built America

Money Power and Wall Street

Plunder: Crime of the Century

The Ascent of Money: A Financial
History of the World

The Spill

Food Matters

Forks over Knives

Food Inc.

Genetic Roulette

Vanishing of the Bees

Farmageddon

Gasland

The Service, another book by Kurt Lewis Allen, graphically illustrates through a series of snapshots in time what the world could look like with the service-oriented truly democratic government suggested in *"Common Sense of Contemporary American Economics and Politics."*

ABOUT THE AUTHOR

Kurt Allen grew up in the small town of Crockett, California, where he graduated from John Swett High School in 1970. He spent just over eight years on active duty in the Air Force before attending college at the University of Puget Sound in Tacoma Washington where he graduated with a Bachelor Degree in Business Administration in 1984. Kurt retired in 2003 after thirty-two years of Federal Service.

ABOUT THE BOOK

The largest amount of America's money is in the hands of a very small portion of the population. This minority, through the use of their money, has gained control of government and industry, to the detriment of the majority. *Common Sense of Contemporary American Economics and Politics* explains what is going on and what we the majority can do about it.